The Family on Pilgrimage

"God Leads Through Dead Ends"

Francis Etheredge

ENROUTE
Make the time

En Route Books and Media, LLC
5705 Rhodes Avenue
St. Louis, MO 63109

Cover credit: TJ Burdick

Library of Congress Control Number: 2018949184

ISBN-10: 1-7324148-3-1
ISBN-13: 978-1-7324148-3-9

DEDICATION

I dedicate this book to my eleven children, three of whom are in heaven, my wife Catherine and to all who have helped to bring this sinner home!

Contents

ACKNOWLEDGMENTS

I would like thank all those who have enriched this book with their testimony: Alberto Gutierrez, Corinna Turner, Alan Soares, Clare Hill, Dominic Quirke, those monks, priests and religious who have given us their prayerful help, particularly those of Parkminster and Prinknash Abbey, the many Catechists who have helped us over the years and the many many others who, in one way or another, have shared our journeys!

“The Flight into Egypt”

Prologue[1]

Beginning with a picture of the Holy Family[2] makes explicit that just as the early life of Christ was generally hidden in the Holy Family of Jesus, Mary and Joseph, so the life of the Holy Family is generally hidden in the pilgrimage of the family. In many ways, especially through the word of God, the life and Liturgy of the Church and prayer, the Holy Family accompanies us throughout our family life[3]; indeed, it might be said, the growth of holiness in the family is a sign of the extent to which the Holy Family accompanies us. Just as the Holy Family is not an unattainable ideal but a "concrete" work of grace, let us not underestimate the need to turn our lives into a meditation on their help[4].

---

[1] I am indebted to Mr. Martin Higgins for his help with proofreading.

[2] By Cosmè Tura (Cosimo di Domenico di Bonaventura) (Italian, Ferrara ca. 1433–1495 Ferrara), courtesy of the generally copyright free New York Metropolitan Library.

[3] The relationship between Judaism and Christianity's expression of the family is explored in Chapter 13: The Holy Family, Celibacy and Marriage: On the "Passage" from the Jewish Rite of Marriage to the Christian Sacrament of Marriage (in *Volume III-Faith is Married Reason*, of the trilogy *From Truth and truth* (Newcastle upon Tyne: Cambridge Scholars Publishing, 2016)).

[4] Cf. Dr. Richard Fitzgibbons, MD, "Children of Divorce: Conflicts and Healing": 'St. Joseph as another loving father who was always present, Our Lady as another loving mother, the Holy Family as one's other stable loving family, and the Lord as one's best friend and brother during painful experiences of the past' (http://www.hprweb.com/2017/03/children-of-divorce-conflicts-and-healing/#comments).

Marriage, parenting, work, hospitality and the needs of the home are all common concerns and, not infrequently, prayers are needed for one or all aspects of this reality: not just for ourselves - but for the many and widespread needs of the society in which we live. Thus, concretely, it may be that the prayer of the family "grows" to the extent that it extends to all aspects of marriage and family life, taking wider and wider sections of society into account as we see, day by day, the need to seek the help of the Holy Family more and more. Whether it is the relationships, the development of a healthy and happy culture, sharing meals and chores, education and talents, going out and being in, transmitting what we have received as well as receiving what the children have to give, the need to pray together as well as the need to go out together, there is no end to the growth of particular and more widely encompassing prayers for the good of the whole human family.

Pilgrimage, then, is a part of this whole growth of the family culture through prayer, games, outings, sport, work, meals, music, books, drawing, homework, household work, films, stories, humour and the welcome of others. Pilgrimage, therefore, is an expression of our social reality as we travel together in our relationship to God; indeed, if it is a part of our lives to ponder questions, then it is a part of our lives to seek and to share our answers. There are many questions. Does God exist? Why pray? Does He answer prayer? Is God male? What if I do not believe in Him? Thus there are the questions about all aspects of the life that we lead; indeed, as frequently as we discuss what arises, there is a need to pray, increasingly, about what is a helpful answer[5].

In a word, just as we turn 'to the "places" in which God has chosen to "pitch his tent" among us (Jn 1:14; cf. Ex 40:34-35; 1 Kgs 8:10-13)'[6], so we turn to the Holy Family as the "unique" place of this encounter.

The First Pilgrim?

Thinking, then, about what a pilgrimage is, gives rise, too, to a question: Who was the first pilgrim? Pilgrim seems to entail two complementary ideas: 'wandering over a distance' and 'journeys made ... [for among other reasons] to discharge some religious obligation'[7]. On the basis of a "religious wandering", it could be argued that Noah and his wife and family (cf. Gn 6: 9-8: 19), Abram, his wife Sarai 'and Lot his brother's son, and all their possessions which they had gathered, and the persons that they had gotten in Haran' (Gn 12: 5) were indeed the first pilgrims. But then, considering that Adam and Eve were driven out of the 'garden of Eden, to till the ground from which ... [Adam] was taken' (Gn 3: 23) it is possible that pilgrimage entered, as it were, the very being of man, male and female, as they were sent from the

---

[5] Cf. Chapter 2 and then Chapter 1 of *The Human Person: A Bioethical Word* (St. Louis, MO: En Route Books and Media, 2017): http://enroutebooksandmedia.com/bioethicalword/.

[6] St. John Paul II, "Concerning Pilgrimage to the Places Linked to the History of Salvation", 1999: http://w2.vatican.va/content/john-paul-ii/en/letters/1999/documents/hf_jp-ii_let_30061999_pilgrimage.html.

[7] Jarrett, Bede. "Pilgrimages." The Catholic Encyclopedia. Vol. 12. New York: Robert Appleton Company, 1911. 29 Mar. 2017 <http://www.newadvent.org/cathen/12085a.htm>.

garden of Eden.

Recalling, too, the more specific pilgrimages which developed when people went up to Shiloh, 'year by year ... to worship and to sacrifice to the Lord of hosts' (1 Sam 1: 3), we see that they went up as a family (cf. 1 Sam 1: 1-5). In other words, even in view of all the imperfections of the family (cf. 1 Sam 1: 2-8), it was the family that went to Shiloh. Hannah, Elkanah's second wife, was barren. Hannah, who was persecuted by Elkanah's fertile wife, prayed out of her distress and was heard by the Lord and, in time, conceived and bore Samuel (cf. 1 Sam 1: 6 – 2: 11).

The pilgrimage of the whole family, then, has an ancient provenance[8]. With the modern institution of the World Meeting of Families, in 1994[9], the pilgrimage of the family is enjoying, along with pilgrimage more generally, 'a unique revival'[10].

Pilgrimage and Culture

At the same time, however, as the very history of pilgrimage witnesses, pilgrims both express the religious life of man and generate culture. On the one hand, there is the development of

---

8 Augustin George refers to numerous locations that became the loci of pilgrimages; and, interestingly enough, even the one mentioned as 'the patriarchs ... one real pilgrimage (Gn 35: 1-7), of Jacob, included his whole family ("Pilgrimage", p. 431 of *Dictionary of Biblical Theology,* second edition, London: Geoffrey Chapman, 1982).

9 It was first organized in Rome, Italy, in 1994 by the then Pontifical Council of the Family, and thereafter every three years: https://en.wikipedia.org/wiki/Pontifical_Council_for_the_Family

10 *YOUCAT*, English, translated by Michael J. Miller (San Francisco: Ignatius Press, 2010), paragraph 276.

roads and towns, the geographical, literary and practical expressions of travel, international communication, hospitality and the development of various religious orders[11]. On the other hand, just as there are benefits, so there are the dangers of neglecting the duties of life, the scandal of the sin of the pilgrim, the challenge to international relations of reconciling conflicting uses or claims to places which have come to possess significance for a variety of world religions[12].

Just as there have been ancient pilgrimages going back into the recesses of time and space, so there are modern traditions in many if not all countries of the world; and, in that sense, St. John Paul II came out of a culture in which pilgrimage was still vividly lived[13] and which was an integral part of what expressed Christianity's Polish enculturation. Thus, along with many other gifts to the world, we may "date" the revival of pilgrimage to his pontificate[14]. At the same time, however, as this is a revival of an ancient practice, it is also a much needed meeting between peoples and cultures and a sign to the modern world of the heart's apprehension of the hidden possibilities of faith for the good of

---

[11] Cf. Jarrett, Bede. "Pilgrimages." The Catholic Encyclopedia.

[12] Cf. Jarrett, Bede. "Pilgrimages." The Catholic Encyclopedia.

[13] Cf. George Weigel, *Witness to Hope: The Biography of Pope John Paul II*, (New York: Cliff Street Books, an imprint of HarperCollins*Publishers*, 1999), p. 305.

[14] Cf. George Weigel, *The End and the Beginning: Pope John Paul II – The Victory of Freedom, the Last Years, the Legacy*, New York etc: Doubleday, 2010, p. 196. Incidentally, the first World Youth Day pilgrimage, grew out of St. John Paul's pastoral desire to accompany the youth of today (cf. George Weigel, *Witness to Hope*, p. 493). The World Youth Days seem to grow out of a number of meetings, beginning in 1984 (cf. http://worldyouthday.com/about-wyd/wyd-history).

society and the salvation of the world.

Perhaps, in a small way, this book can contribute to the revival of the pilgrimage for the layman, those seeking out their vocation and indeed for the living out of family life as an expression of the 'domestic church' (*Lumen Gentium,* 11): the Gospel's opening embrace of both the temporal and the eternal "family of man". Let us embrace the 'inner pilgrimage'[15] from love to love and, when possible, its outward expression in the life of the Church.

Pilgrimage and Human Identity

In this sense, pilgrimage is both an expression of the 'religious sense of the Christian people'[16] and an expression of the very reality of Christian personhood: that we are a pilgrim people; indeed, as the *Youth Catechism of the Catholic Church* says: 'Someone who goes on a pilgrimage "prays with his feet" and experiences with all his senses that his entire life is one long journey to God'[17]. Furthermore, as it says in *Lumen Gentium* (the Light of the Nations), the document on the Church of the Second Vatican Council, 'the pilgrim Church, in its sacraments and institutions, which belong to this present age, carries the mark of this world which will pass, and she herself takes her place among the creatures which groan and travail yet and await the revelation

---

[15] Pope Francis: "Pope's Letter to World Meeting of Families in Dublin 2018", 25 March, 2017; https://zenit.org/articles/popes-letter-for-world-meeting-of-families-in-dublin/.

[16] *Catechism of the Catholic Church,* (CCC), 1674.

[17] *YOUCAT,* 276, which references the *Catechism of the Catholic Church,* 1674.

of the sons of God (cf. Rom. 8: 19-22)' (48). In other words, the very mission of the Church is both to transform this fallen world with the fruits of redemption, which include our "leavened" labour (cf. *Lumen Gentium*, 36), while recognizing that even what is temporal points to an eternal destiny (cf. *Gaudium et Spes*, 39); and, therefore, just as marriage is a temporal vocation, so it also points to the eschatological goal of man 'so that, when the single course of our earthly life is completed (cf. Heb. 9: 27), we may merit to enter with him into the marriage feast and be numbered among the blessed (cf. Mt. 25: 31-46)' (*Lumen Gentium*, 48).

Pilgrimage and the Proclamation of Faith in Jesus Christ

In the final part of this Prologue I have decided to include another person's experience of evangelization; and, more generally, there is a variety of other people's experiences in the book as a whole. This expresses the "social" nature of evangelization and pilgrimage; but, more particularly, it addresses the relationship between evangelization and the Christian Life. Although I had grown up in a Catholic family there came a "moment" when a dialogue with Len, a member of Marriage Encounter, a movement dedicated to the renewal of marriage, led me towards the Neocatechumenal Way, a modern charism of the Catholic Church. The Neocatechumenal Way is a formation in the Christian Faith which draws on the Liturgy, the Word of God and the Community. This "moment", then, was when I was neither married, nor a priest, nor a monk nor anything. Indeed, all the attempts that I had made to find a vocation had come to nothing. Even in terms of natural talents, I was unable to finish any courses, find congenial work or really to make progress with the basic characteristics of life. This was not a fleeting problem but a moment full of pain: a moment that had included the joy of fathering a child which had then turned to an indescribable agony on listening to the mother who told me of the abortion of our child.

Len, then, told me about a priest who was open to a wide range of modern movements in the Church; and, I said to myself, I would go and visit this parish Church if he told me once more about it: he did; I went. There was nothing automatic about discovering the reality of the Christian Faith; and, at one point, I remember rebelling against the possibility that I had no faith. But, in fact, this was my reality and, as you will see in the course of this book, going from living a restless life to becoming a conscious pilgrim was very much about encountering the truth about myself that exceeded simple psychological insight.

I have included Alberto's experience of evangelizing at this point, then, as a way of acknowledging the many people who, in one way or another, came to help me encounter the reality of Jesus Christ and His Church; and, just as many of them may never know the effect that they have had on my life, so Alberto may never know the effect that he has had on the people he encountered. Let us not forget, then, that there is a love of God in the preaching: a preaching that comes with the possibility of begetting a beginning to the life of faith (cf. Rom 10: 14-17)[18]. Catechists came to the parish priest, who then invited me to come to a catechesis, who

[18] As you will discover in the course of this book, however, my own gift of faith came through reading a particular passage in the *Catechism of the Catholic Church*.

then brought me into contact with people who began, very actively, to pray for me and to invite me to faith. We are, then, a part of a procession or even a pilgrimage of faith that goes back to the Old Testament and, taking a new beginning in Jesus Christ, continues into the present.

Alberto Gutierrez: An Experience of Evangelization[19]

My name is Alberto Gutierrez, I am forty seven years old and I come from Burgos, Spain. I am the youngest of eight brothers and my parents were a family in mission in Peru for sixteen years. I married Arancha eighteen years ago. We do not have any children. I studied law in Spain and I worked as an accountant. I am currently a Catholic missionary in Cheltenham, England, and have been so for the last six years. My mission is to announce the love of God and to support communities from the Neocatechumenal Way. My job is to care for children with special needs and I give Spanish lessons.

My Experience of a 2 x 2

This week of evangelization has been a time of great grace and peace. Since I started I felt that Jesus Christ was with me all the time, and the Virgin Mary, especially when we prayed the Rosary. At night, suddenly I awoke and began to pray without effort as something natural.

[19] I am very grateful for the biographies and experiences which now adorn this book; they are generally presented as they have been received except for minor typographical or literary changes.

My Armour

The Cross, The Bible, The Divine Office, The Rosary, a map, my companion Fernando and the prayer of all the other evangelizers, those praying for us in our communities and in monasteries.

The Place

We were walking in the suburbs of London and, without exception, we loved everyone whom we saw during our mission.

When it Started

I started this week of evangelization with fear, in precariousness, without money, mobile phone, a change of clothes, identity cards ... unworthy to do this great mission. I have a low level of spoken English.

When it Ended

At the end I was the happiest man on earth: happy; happy; happy! I saw how the Lord provided for us at all times, in the most irrelevant things. Without asking, some people helped us to get to the houses of the priests we planned to visit: a gardener; a postman ... angels. We walked, walked and walked. I do not like to walk. I was completely tired but happy to walk for my faith if not for my health. When the mission ended my catechist washed my feet. In this moment, I remembered each face, each step, each suffering in the name of God. How many miracles. The devil was completely without power.

The Kerygma

This Kerygma is the best news that a man can listen to.

Jesus Christ has died for you, for me, He died on a cross, He is the only just one; He has given all of His life, until the last drop of His blood, out of an infinite love for you and for me.

And He loves us even if we are poor sinners. He is waiting, always, for us. I love you, I love you as you are, when you are happy, when you are sad, or when you have a serious illness that you do not understand, or when you are unavailable to love your husband, your wife, your children, your family, your boss, your friends, because they are not as you would like them to be. Jesus Christ is in every situation in your life. Nothing is by chance. Jesus Christ is there. He is the only one who knows your sufferings; in these crosses He is loving you. Everything is new with Him: A new life; a new creature. Everything has sense, lived from the love of Christ. Christ is really risen! This is the Kerygma, amazing!

I have begun to live the Kerygma, not as a theory but as something real; it is the best news to experience in your own body, in your own soul, the immense love of Jesus Christ. I spoke about this with the priests we visited.

We Went to 18 Parish Priests

The important thing, according to me, was that when we were rejected by 6 parish priests, more or less suddenly, without effort, we were brought to love these priests and to pray especially for them during our mission.

Another 6 priests listened to the Kerygma to be polite or courteous.

Then there were 6 priests who listened very carefully to the Kerygma. I have not the words to describe how some of their faces changed during the announcement of the Kerygma, but they were really happy.

The Face of God

I saw the Face of God in a man without a face. His name was Simon. Cancer had destroyed his face. He had no nose and in its place was a piece of white plastic and he was blind in the left eye.

Simon is a tall man, an English non-practicing Catholic, with a dog.

The Situation

At 22:00 Fernando and I were really tired. It was the Feast of St. James and we had walked around 15 miles. We had not eaten and no one offered hospitality. We asked for food in a Spanish restaurant and we ate a Spanish dinner; afterwards, we went to sleep in the middle of a park.

At this moment, in the total darkness, we heard a dog and Simon came over to us and asked: "Who are you? Are you drinking?" We answered: "We are Catholic missionaries. We are announcing the Good News to Parish Priests". Simon asked: "And what is this mission?" We answered: "Because the priest is not here we announce to you the Good News". Fernando and I started to announce the Kerygma and he accepted very, very well the love of God. He said: "Are you two angels?" We answered: "No. We are normal people". Simon said: "Sorry; but this place is dangerous for you, because this place is the meeting point for bubbles, drug addicts .... Ok; follow me and I will show you the best place in this area to sleep".

Simon was surprised because we were without money, food ....

At 22:30, we started to sleep all night under two great trees, but suddenly Simon appeared with a bag full of food. We had an English dinner. He offered us 20 pounds but, in a friendly way, we refused the money. We spoke with him for 15 minutes. I think that he was happy with us or worried. He went home.

At 23:15, Simon appeared with a sleeping bag for us, a mat, a big piece of plastic to protect us in case it started to rain and two plastic chairs. We arrived without anything and in this moment it was similar to a camping place. We spoke with him for 10 minutes. He went home.

At 24:00, Simon appeared again with two familiar Domino pizzas: an Italian Dinner. We talked for 1 hour. He knew a city from Spain, Burgos, because his first girlfriend was from Burgos. The other funny aspect to this was that his job was a guard for festivals. We said to him: "You are the guardian angel"; he was with us until 1:10 am. He was at all times happy and worried about our situation; finally, he went home. But before going home he said: "To end this day we need to pray" and he started to pray the Our Father, with his arms lifted and with complete joy. Fernando and I were surprised and his joy was contagious.

I am sure that this night was the best experience in our mission.

Saint John Paul II

Courtesy of Wikipedia

General Introduction

Part I: An Unexpected Beginning

No doubt we all have our ideas about how a book should begin; and, already, I have been through a variety of opening lines. Indeed, the book is now introduced with a prologue on pilgrimage which, in an unexpected way, confirmed the theme of the family on pilgrimage. In addition, I have now included a "moment" of evangelization; for, on reflection, each of us experiences a kind of transmission of what we have received.

Why, then, have I decided to begin with a reference to what is unexpected? The unexpected, then, comes with a word: a word about the unexpected "moment" of death; and, therefore, as death impacts on us all, it is a good point of departure: a glimpsed opening on the mystery of passing through life to life eternal. On the one hand, pilgrimage is a part of the on-going patrimony of mankind; and, on the other hand, it is lived afresh and personally in the life of each pilgrim and family.

An Unexpected Point of Departure

Although I was concerned about my chest, the doctor was examining my swollen, red and blotchy leg; and, following a blood test for the presence of clotting, the result was 14 when a more normal response was 0.35: an enormous difference. Thus I was sent for an ultrasound scan on the top of my leg. But for a bit of pulsing blue and white past a dark grey mass, the vein was almost completely blocked. I was very impressed with the technology that enabled us to see what was happening in my veins, but I felt a bit wobbly as I came out of the ultra sound examination of a clot in my right leg: the clot was the length of the whole leg.

I am married and we have eight children and, therefore, the news of the clotting has an impact on us all. Will I see the maturing of our younger children, the vocational choices of our older ones or the graduation of our eldest? Indeed, will it matter? If I enter eternal life before my wife and children, I will be their advocate with the Lord; and, indeed, press every other concern I have for the welfare of others and our planet. In a recent celebration of the Eucharist, this early warning of the possibility of death is an invitation to see that Christ is coming to meet me. On the one hand, this is wonderfully good and encouraging news; but, on the other hand, the traces of fear encourage me to make ready with the repentance which belongs to Lent and the hope that belongs to Easter[20].

---

[20] The tests continued with a chest scan, detecting old clots and an enlarged right side of the heart compensating for the extra work. Following the CT scan, an abdominal ultra sound scan revealed that the prostate gland, which needed surgery a few years ago owing to it being so enlarged, is still grossly enlarged but

Pilgrims throughout Time

This is not a unique experience and many of us, I am sure, encounter those "moments" when death is not a skull on the desk or a remote possibility; but, for one reason or another, death is vividly present and challenges us to recognize our "pilgrim" calling: that we are "en route" through this life. Indeed, that the whole of humanity is on a vast passage through the vortex of time to eternity; and, if it is possible, I hope that passing from this life involves passing through the utter reaches of the universe to marvel, once more, at the magnificent splendour of creation before, finally, meeting the Creator. These events remind us that our lives are uncertain and unpredictably long or short; and, in whatever way it is genuinely possible, the word of love is what remains: to live and leave a legacy of love.

Pilgrims World-Wide and the Word of God

There are, indeed, many people who, in their distress and even agony, are fleeing from one country to another in the hope of a welcome; and, indeed, there are all kinds of other hardships and difficulties which invite us to ask the question: What is God saying to me throughout the problems I am experiencing in my life? In this sense, then, perhaps a pilgrimage is not just about the fact

---

not cancerous. Several months after beginning a course of anti-coagulant medicine, there is now a disturbing but not unknown development of slight internal bleeding. Thus the tests and treatments continue. I must, therefore, record my gratitude to our *National Health Service* and to our doctors and staff, particularly the doctor who is seeing through this very thorough investigation of the presenting symptoms.

that we all experience hardship in daily life, in the journey from the slavery of Egypt to the freedom of the Promised Land or in the passage from death to life, from falsehood to truth and from hatred to love. But a pilgrimage is when we are increasingly conscious that a question is being posed: What is God saying to me in this event of my life? This is the on-going pilgrimage of life in which we constantly encounter the meaning of our experience in the context of the embracing word of God: the journey that we are called to make and which is, constantly, about returning to the beginning, to listening (cf. Dt 6: 3-9) and to beginning again.

Pilgrimage, then, can be about the journey we make to find who we are, whether throughout our lives or in the particular "moments" of crisis, homelessness or illness; but, more generally, it is about that search for meaning which, in the end, is a journey into the mystery of God and His Word: witnessing to the existence of God, to the help of His Word and the Church and to the hope that we all need to live through the difficulties we experience.

Part II: A Comment on the Structure of the Work as a Whole

Bringing a collection of essays together on the theme of the family on pilgrimage opens up a new question: What is a pilgrimage? Even the title image, as it were, of the Holy Family's Flight from Egypt can make us ask: In what way do we participate in the world's afflictions? Indeed, is a pilgrimage primarily about the difficulties being encountered? Discovering what we have in common with the world's hardships helps us in our experience of solidarity and, therefore, our common prayer and action. Whether it was the time when our family was unable to go on living with my aging mother and, being poor, studying and ill, it was a "moment" to move, three times, until we arrived at our present home. Or it was unemployment, illness or sufferings in the family, which were and are the experiences of the need for good counsel, prayer and the help of others. All of this "experience" is a part of that passage from pride to humility, isolationism to welcoming support and discovering the word through others which "re-lives" the word we receive through the lives of others in the Scripture. Thus the unexpected changes of life or the "echo" of other lives can bring with them that question and its challenging examination of conscience: Can I bless God today?

Pilgrimage, however, entails that more straightforward sense of deliberately entering into that time of travelling in the Lord's presence; and, given that the Church is a community of travellers, it is a time of travelling "in caravan" and breaking and sharing the word and the Word of the Eucharist. At the same time, however, we may have begun our pilgrimages single, unmarried and even unmarriageable; but, in view of coming to our vocational decision, once married, we may well have continued on these journeys with, or at times without, our growing number of children. Thus this book is also about encouraging a family to go on pilgrimage and, even if at times it is impractical, impossible and even precarious, it is an experience which the Lord leads: an experience that helps us to see that the Lord always leads.

A more specific comment on the structure of the book

In wondering about how to begin, because most of these accounts were written after I had been married a while and, possibly, could give the impression of a life that "fell together", I have decided to start with a group of poems, part of which is a cycle of poems about change. Change, in this cycle of poems, is that almost involuntary process that springs from the impulse to be what we are – which unsettles everything constantly until, in some sense, what we are begins to be "lived" in what we do. In addition, I hope to show how writing is a part of this process of pilgrimage; indeed, just as there is a pilgrimage from England to Israel, so there is a pilgrimage from frustration to fulfilment: to that way of living out the reality of what we are which takes account of the whole gift of human personhood and not just "parts" of it.

There now follows a General Introduction to each particular chapter, which both serves to give an overview of the contents of each and every chapter and thus of the book as a whole and, at the same time, each of them is used again at the beginning of each chapter in the hope of reminding the reader of where it is going. This differs from the Introduction to each chapter, which was originally written as a part of that particular essay. In other words, each General Introduction to a chapter is written more recently and enables a revisiting of it in the light of bringing the book as a whole to exist.

Part III: A General Introduction to Each Particular Chapter

General Introduction to Chapter 1: An Unconscious Pilgrim Becoming Conscious. If the contents of this chapter include "The Life-Cycle Prose-Poems" then why begin with a piece of prose; and, indeed, a piece of prose that ranges over twenty years of marriage and family life? The reason is simple: it was when writing that account of our twentieth wedding anniversary that it began to dawn on me how much my life, my married and family life even more so, was structured on a pattern of pilgrimages. In other words, without going into a lengthy autobiography, this prose account and these poems give an account of "where I am coming from" and, therefore, they refer to the living context of pilgrimages: the life-purposes or their frustration out of which arises the need for pilgrimage. At the same time, however, the whole book is entitled "The Family on Pilgrimage"; and, therefore, although this book looks at the context of the life out of which pilgrimages have arisen, part two of this chapter gives a more expanded account of a particular family pilgrimage.

Thus this chapter naturally divides into three parts: an overview of marriage and family life; a family pilgrimage; and the perspective of poems that root those accounts in a fuller account of the lived experience of being an unconscious pilgrim: an unconscious pilgrim in search of an elusive self that is perhaps self-deceptively self-preoccupied with self-discovery.

General Introduction to Chapter 2: In Pilgrimage to the Coming of the Word. In the three parts of this chapter there are almost three steps towards the Word's coming.

In the first step there is the occasional poem, written at different times, in the course of my theological studies. At the same time, however, I recall that although I had begun the study of theology, it did not follow that a conversion of heart or an understanding of faith was at the root of it; indeed, this time entailed, as at other times, falling into sin and seeking confession: a kind of faltering following of Christ which, in reality, implied the power of human weakness to be powerfully present and active. In retrospect, it is clearer now than it was then, that the call to conversion can be relatively shallow: a growing recognition of the reasons for beginning to hate the weakness of the flesh; but, at the same time, a kind of powerlessness in the face of it indicating a deeply addictive attraction to the sins of the flesh. There was a certain devotionalism, too, almost a tangible consciousness of the presence of Christ in the Eucharist. But, like a free electron out of the orbit of the nucleus, I was unable to fight off the attraction to sin – the unwrapping of the gift not completely given being stronger than the repulsing remembrance of the agonies which followed. Nevertheless, in the midst of this time, there emerged a growing attraction to the Church if for no other reason than the teachings of the Church, particularly of the popes, began to appeal to me: how well structured they were; brief, incisive and yet comprehensive accounts of reality; and, either explicitly or implicitly, expressing and raising real and challenging questions.

The second step, charted in Part II, brings out the more radical conversion to Christ through the moment of rejection: a rejection by Christ. I remember, in other words, as I began to see the good qualities of the Church in a rather impersonal way, such as the growth of small communities and a new emphasis on the Word of God, so I entered more fully into a superficial relationship to the Church: a kind of rational attraction to the goodness of it while, at the same time, resisting the recognition of being a sinner. Thus there came a point when, finally, I found myself in the Gospel of the wedding feast – as the man thrown out as he had not come in wedding garments (cf. Mt 22: 1-14 [esp. 11-14]); and, in a newly radical way, I experienced the whole event of sin as a real wretchedness that led to contemplating suicide – to which Christ came with a word of hope from the *Catechism of the Catholic Church*.

The third and final step of this chapter is a reflection that looks at the diverse gifts of pilgrimage; indeed, pilgrimage implies but does not state so explicitly, that there is an almost involuntary witness to the help of God. In other words, given the many difficulties encountered in the course of fundraising, travel and accommodation, a pilgrimage is a concrete witness to us, and therefore through us, to the providential help of God. At the same time, however, the help of God is present throughout life and needs an occasion to make it more visible; and, therefore, it is about proclaiming the deeds of God as well as experiencing them in a variety of ways.

Thus this chapter has three parts. Part I: Three Poems: Our Mother of the Incarnation; Bread of Love, Wine of Glory; and Christmas; Part II: A Prose account of the Enlightening Work of the Word of God; and Part III: The Gifts of Pilgrimage.

<u>*General Introduction to Chapter 3:*</u> A World Youth Day Pilgrimage, 2016. In a certain sense this pilgrimage began in an Anglican Abbey, although one older than the Reformation, in a chapel dedicated to Our Lady and, more than a year later, ended with a prayer of thanks in that same chapel. While on the first occasion there were the other pilgrims with whom we were fundraising and travelling, not even ourselves having decided to go yet, on the second occasion there were several from our family and the remembrance, on visiting this chapel again, that we had in fact been to Poland and back. Thus, as I recall the time we spent fundraising, traversing Europe and the visit with Pope Francis in Cracow, I am inclined to think that this pilgrimage was in fact a gift of Mary: even an ecumenical gift of Mary. A pilgrimage, then, is often about more than we realise; and, therefore, I am sure it was also about our relationship to Mary, Mother of the Lord and to Joseph, her spouse. In a certain sense, then, a pilgrimage is about our relationship to the whole Holy Family who are, I am sure, accompanying us in our pilgrimage through family life and all that makes it up: both the ordinary and the extraordinary events of life. Perhaps, too, in view of the growing rediscovery of the "mystery" of Mary, Mother of the Lord, perhaps the Holy Family is central to modern ecumenism.

But, more prosaically, even in the event of finding it difficult to fix a towel rail in the bathroom, having tried various styles, I have prayed to St. Joseph and then "invented" a construction which took advantage of the weak fixing and used hanging flower basket brackets and tubes between them to make a reasonably lasting place for some of the several towels to hang. More importantly, then, there are innumerable times that I have turned to St. Joseph to teach me how to be a helpful spouse and father. Likewise I remind the children of the childhood of Christ and, I am sure, of the generosity of His parents in looking after other people (cf. Mt 12: 47). Thus their family life informs our actual daily life in all kinds of ways.

Part I is about how and why we raised the money and went on pilgrimage with over three hundred others and around two and a half million more (I). The next two pieces give an overview of the pilgrimage to Cracow (II) and a more specific account of a reflection on Edith Stein, based on a catechesis which I gave, as "her gift to me", in a Carmelite Monastery in Czerna, Poland (III).

General Introduction to Chapter 4: Traversing Life. There comes a point, then, when being an unconscious pilgrim changed, whether or not through actual pilgrimages, and I began to see that I needed the help of God; indeed that death, whatever kind of doorway it will be, helps us to recognize that we are a part of a great exodus: a passing of people from slavery to freedom: from being estranged from others to being fit for friendship: from an unwillingness to live forgiveness to love's possibility of the gift of eternal life. Thus there is, as it were, a passage to being a pilgrim. On the one hand this book charts, in a way, the very passage to pilgrimage: from an almost inbuilt restlessness to consciously hoping in the Word of God; but, on the other hand, this particular chapter takes us through the traversal of a life that shows, as clearly as life-changes can, that becoming a pilgrim enables us to see that God "completes" the work of "becoming ourselves". It is not as if the hardships will necessarily cease, or indeed the need to pray come to an end, but it is at least clear that life is going towards eternity. Or to put it the other way round: we are being drawn through time to eternity.

One of "life's-questions", as it were, is whether or not to marry, to be a monk or a priest; and, as it transpires, a central theme of this pilgrimage from a multitude of uncertainties was, in fact, being able to marry and to unfold a family life. At the same time, as we shall see in the final chapter, another of "life's-questions" is what work belongs to me to do: a question that ran throughout the years of the Life-Cycle prose-poems and continues to call me to pray and to work. A third question, inseparable to the other two and more prominently expressed in this chapter is the relationship between vocation and conversion: conversion brought clarity about vocation.

This chapter begins, then, with a personal history of coming to marriage: of coming to marriage through all kinds of suffering (I). Secondly, there is a more developed exploration of how experience informs our understanding of the accompaniment that is so frequently necessary to people returning to the sacrament of matrimony or indeed being embraced by it (II). Finally, there is how to make sense of one of the ongoing questions in our time: Is there a real human nature and how does it express itself in "influencing" our concrete choices (III)?

General Introduction to Chapter 5: The Vocation to Write. It has taken an interminably long time to get to the point of writing full-time; and, I am sure, a part of what has made the journey so long are all the courses, work and family demands which have been an inbuilt part of long-term daily life. Nevertheless, without this enormous experience of everyday life I would be a very different person and a very different writer; and, therefore, this is not about lamenting what did not happen but, rather, reflecting on what does happen: what the Lord in His wisdom is even now permitting to be possible. There is a line in one of the psalms which sums up, in a way, the possibilities of life which remain in the hands of the Lord to unfold, even in our later years: 'They still bring forth fruit in old age, they are ever full of sap and green' (Ps 92: 14); and, what is more, that this fruitful old age is a sign of the presence of the Lord: 'to show that the Lord is upright; he is my rock, and there is no unrighteousness in him' (Ps 92: 15).

In one sense, then, this present season of writing arose after completing a book on the uniqueness of Scripture while still commuting to work; but, on beginning to write the second book, it became clear that there was too much material for one and therefore it became a trilogy on faith and reason. Thus, while there were other factors, it seemed as if the Lord was offering an opportunity to write. Then there was the disappointment of the very promising terms of the trilogy book contract realising nothing in the way of an income as the books did not sell in a way which helped us. Thus there has been a period of exploring other outlets with short articles, poems and a period of ongoing experimentation with business social media; but, again, while this generated some interest it has not automatically translated into commercial success. Nevertheless, though, all this experience has contributed to the "log", as it were, of the vocation of the writer and now constitutes a contribution to this final chapter on pilgrimage.

Pilgrimage, then, includes the whole life-long search for the vocational work which would both be fulfilling and contribute, as it can, to the search for truth which is so urgently needed in our times: a search which needs to investigate the foundations of human personhood in order the better to explain the nature of human action and the mystery of the human person as a "being-in-relation". At the same time, as these pages have indicated, writing is not about totally abstracting what is written from everyday life. There is a sense, therefore, that the thread of experience that has run through earlier work and is now increasingly evident in this one, is a part of the task of communicating more wholesomely the reality of conversion and its implications in the concrete facts of a particular life. Thirdly, though, the vocation of the writer is a vocation to communicate as widely as possible: to appeal to the everyday "person" concerning the profound crises of human identity and action which confront us "today". In a way, then, this book and this chapter are still about seeking the fulfilment of that vision and, at the same time, striving to meet the everyday needs of marriage and family life. In other words, the call to work is as alive today as it ever was; and, in so far as it continues to bear little financial fruit, so this work has to undergo changes that mature the vision while, at the same time, it engages more and more realistically with the task of providing a living that even in this late hour I still hope to contribute.

The pilgrimage of work, then, I hope will help to illuminate the choices that our children will make as they go into adult life.

This chapter is formed of three parts and charts, first through an earlier poem and piece of prose and a more recent prose poem (I), then later through a summary account of the most recent period of self-employment (II) and, finally, through a further reflection on writing itself - how the work of a writer is yet an on-going gift and task to be accepted and undertaken afresh (III).

In the second experience which complements this work as a whole, there is a pilgrimage to a shrine in our own country and its relationship to the work of a new religious congregation.

Corinna Turner

Corinna Turner is a British Catholic author, Lay Dominican and occasional journalist. Her novel 'Liberation' was nominated for the Carnegie Medal Award 2016 and her books have also been placed in the Catholic Arts and Letters Award and the Catholic Press Awards. Her main published work is the 'I Am Margaret' series (Catholic dystopian novels for young adults and adults). Corinna has been writing since she was fourteen and likes strong protagonists with plenty of integrity. She was raised Methodist, migrated to the Anglicans, and finally swam the Tiber in 2010!

Corinna Turner: A Pilgrimage to Walsingham and its Relationship to a New Religious Congregation and to Providence

The pilgrimage began with Mass in the grand old remains of the ruined abbey in Bury St Edmunds, now a public garden. Passers-by watched our open air proceedings with curiosity; the wind tried to carry our gazebo away and two young men had to stand for the rest of the consecration, holding it down over the altar. Then back to the school at which we were staying, for evening meal and introductions.

We'd come from all over the country to take part in the St John

Paul II Pilgrimage for the New Evangelisation of England and Wales, which was started, and is still run by the Dominican Sisters of St Joseph, a comparatively new—and growing—congregation based in the New Forest.

After night prayer, we bedded down for the night, the ladies in the school hall, the guys in the converted crypt. Most of us slept reasonably, except for Joanna Bogle whose airbed proved faulty. Not the best thing to discover on night one!

In the morning, we piled into every available vehicle for the transfer to our actual starting point, the village of Brandon, where the congregation of the local Catholic church waited to provide Mass—and breakfast! Waffles, berry-laden syrup, pastries... truthfully it wasn't remotely Friday-fare, but it got us off to a good start!

Most un-abstemiously replete, we finally waddled on our way. Having offered to navigate, I was up front with the pace-setter, a not particularly tall lady who earned the nick-name 'the machine' because of her indomitable, relentless progress. Truly, she performed a tremendous service to the pilgrimage by keeping us moving and on time, no matter how tired we became.

Heading across open country and into Thetford Forest in glorious sunshine that persisted for the entire weekend, we passed pig farms and quaint churches, and tantalising signs to old hill forts... but this was a pilgrimage, and we could not indulge in private explorations and diversions. Before long we found the support vehicle waiting for us, to provide our first break. Cereal bars and water were on hand, along with an honest-to-goodness portaloo in its own little tent.

I was bemused by this to begin with, but soon learned the

rationale behind it. In earlier years, the pilgrimage had stopped at various houses along the route for occasional 'comfort breaks', dolling out thank you boxes of chocolates to the obliging home owners. But with the numbers of pilgrims swelling to forty or fifty, and the houses boasting only one or perhaps two conveniences each, it became impractically time-consuming. A portaloo, set up and waiting at every breakpoint, kept things from degenerating into one long exercise in the development of patience!

Lunch was DIY sandwiches, and everyone sat down to eat as the ten miles began to make themselves felt—and the thought of another ten before evening. But the Camino it wasn't, and our heads knew that even if our legs didn't. After all, our luggage had already arrived at our next overnight destination, borne hither in the hired minibus, and Sister Julie and Sister Mary Benedicta were already hard at work cooking a delicious evening meal.

All the same, most of us were not especially fit, myself included, and we were hobbling by the time we reached Swaffham, where we were staying at a Catholic school. There were two gyms in this school, so men and women had similar accommodation. An under-eighteen had also been discovered lurking amongst our ranks, and he had to be isolated in separate accommodation—easy enough at Swaffham, though to prove much more challenging the following night.

In the morning, we were up and off again bright and early. By this time I was feeling glad I was the navigator, because it meant I had to stay at the front. Without this obligation I would surely have been trailing in the rear with the stragglers!

Day two traversed more beautiful terrain—though very distinct from day one—stopping for Mass and lunch at Castle Acre.

Boasting another set of fabulous ruins, Castle Acre has an intact medieval church in which the vicar graciously allowed us to say Mass—probably the first Mass said there in 400 years. Afterwards we enjoyed another picnic in the gloriously sunny graveyard. Some people were uncomfortable tucking in among the headstones, but I couldn't help feeling the deceased would be pleased to have such a cheerful band keeping them company—and a band with their sights set on such a holy goal, after all. Walsingham, and the New Evangelisation of England and Wales!

The odd person actually felt that the pilgrimage was too jolly—and too comfortable. It was gently pointed out that for most of the people there, simply walking twenty miles a day and sleeping on the floor was deprivation of heretofore unexperienced proportions.

We headed out of Castle Acre past another set of magnificent ruins, dissuaded a horse from joining in the pilgrimage, and plodded on. For most of us, the pain was really kicking in. Putting one foot in front of the other became agony. We limped along the edge of a seemingly unending disused airfield—and finally reached our evening destination, the village of Helhoughton. Here, the very kind vicar was allowing us to sleep in the little church hall, and the Anglican church itself. The chaps were exiled to the damp church, the ladies to the cramped hall, and the under-eighteen? After much head scratching and conferring and drawing of blanks, the under-eighteen was domiciled, Harry Potter-style, in a very large cupboard!

By this point, everyone was sleeping soundly at night, hard floors and snoring and unfamiliar surroundings notwithstanding. Morning found us again on our feet, on the road, for the last leg... or possibly on our last legs!

But we made it. We even made it in time to be inserted into the entrance procession for Sunday Mass at the R. C. National Shrine. We prayed in the shrine afterwards, visited the gift shop, enjoyed one last DIY lunch together, then walked the Holy Mile into Walsingham itself. Where, after Benediction in the Catholic church, with great sadness, we split up and went our separate ways, happier and stronger in the faith and much improved by the experience—and thoroughly reminded through our increased awareness of our physical limitations just how much we depend on God.

Saint Teresa of Ávila

Courtesy of Wikipedia

Chapter One

An Unconscious Pilgrim Becomes Conscious

General Introduction to Chapter 1: Becoming Conscious of Being on Pilgrimage. If the contents of this chapter include "The Life-Cycle Prose-Poems" then why begin with a piece of prose; and, indeed, a piece of prose that ranges over twenty years of marriage and family life? The reason is simple: it was when writing that account of our twentieth wedding anniversary that it began to dawn on me how much my life, my married and family life even more so, was structured on a pattern of pilgrimages. In other words, without going into a lengthy autobiography, this prose account and these poems give an account of "where I am coming from" and, therefore, they refer to the living context of pilgrimages: the life-purposes or their frustration out of which arises the need for pilgrimage. At the same time, however, the whole book is entitled "The Family on Pilgrimage"; and, therefore, although this book looks at the context of the life out of which pilgrimages have arisen, part two of this chapter gives a more expanded account of a particular family pilgrimage.

Thus this chapter naturally divides into three parts: an overview of marriage and family life; a family pilgrimage; and the perspective of poems that root those accounts in a fuller account of the lived experience of being an unconscious pilgrim: an unconscious pilgrim in search of an elusive self that is perhaps self-deceptively self-preoccupied with self-discovery.

Part I: A Prose account of the Beads of Pilgrimage

Introduction

Where to begin? I cannot begin with success – but with the failure through which God succeeded in communicating with me. What is more, it was in writing this piece after twenty years of marriage that I realised that pilgrimage, like Holy Beads, ran down the years from then until now.

Marriage: Seven Unplanned Points

I was nearing the completion of a first degree after numerous failed attempts at psychological self-insight, higher education, self-employment, writing and poetry publishing and yet again returned home from a period of intermittent estrangement from my father and mother, brothers and sisters, to live in the basement flat of my parent's house. In the midst of a crisis at forty, instead of suicide, I suddenly believed that just as God could bring all that exists out of nothing, so He could make a new beginning for the sinner (cf. *Catechism of the Catholic Church*, 298). I then went on a pilgrimage to Loreto in Italy and received the word of Christ to the woman caught in adultery: "go, and do not sin again" (Jn 8: 11); and, like the word of creation itself, the word of Christ brought about what it proclaimed - a new beginning.

Within a year, I went out with the woman who was to become my fiancé and we went to see a priest who encouraged us to read the Book of Tobit, who told me to take work and who was a frequent confessor who helped me to live a chaste courtship. I took work as a laundry labourer; and, as such, it helped me and my fiancé to see that this obedience was a sign of the grace of God at work in our lives. When I had been considering the possibility of the priesthood, I had been asked to find work and had found reasons to disregard the advice. Surrounded by the help of others who provided mugs and money, a reception, a honeymoon in a cottage and various other helps to begin a home, we married.

The call to prayer, lived as a daily help, especially the prayer before coming together as man and wife, saw us through our frequent monetary difficulties and a particular time when we could only manage a silent walk. We received a grant for me to write a book and so I resigned from the laundry. My frequent illnesses, including clots in my leg and lungs, pneumonia and pleurisy, the gift of studying for an MA in Catholic Theology, the demands of young children and little money, continued to make daily prayer an absolute necessity.

Then there was the prolonged period of studying course after course, writing unsuccessfully, short term work placements and a growing family. My father had given us his car, not long before he died, as our vehicle had ceased to move on the forecourt of a superstore. We went away, periodically, on weekend retreats, finding that God provided various people to help with our children, whether or not they came with us. As my health was often very uncertain and I was frequently exhausted, lying on the floor and praying for our own home was a "break" from trying to study Hebrew; and, suddenly, my mother sold the house and the whole inconvenience of having to move was transformed into an answer to a prayer as we ended up in a council house big enough for our five children.

By the time our eighth child came along, I had a qualification and teaching experience in higher education and, in answer to a prayer prompt when studying the Our Father, I went to the Church to pray for work. Having by now some public lecturing experience, a few pieces of published writing, we continued to make ends meet with the many and various works of providence. In brief, with four qualifications in higher education, I started work at a college on a very modest salary but with hours that allowed me to be home for dinner with the family and during the children's school holidays.

It is impossible to describe the years of parenthood, still on-going, as the older children start to pass through the "going out" or "doing other things phases"; and, as with everything else, the constant necessity of prayer: for them and for us and for all parents in all the stages of life, education, employment, unemployment, illness and trials of all kinds. Not to mention the many holiday activities, from sliding on cardboard down grassy slopes to helping different children in the many skills and works of home and garden; and, at the same time, there are the million and one conversations about what to do, what games to play at the meal table or, as they get older, what to talk about.

Then there is the whole work of helping the children to understand philosophical concepts, like soul and body, space, time and eternity; and, in addition, to develop the gift of baptism with the word of God, prayer and helping each other to see how it illuminates our lives. In the course of various pilgrimages, we also went to a variety of places and events. We went the round of the United Kingdom when Pope Benedict XVI came to visit, following his itinerary from afar as we could not afford the £1000 we would have needed for the coach travel; but, nevertheless, God provided another car and driver and we went in two cars, more or less following the papal route, only that much slower! Then, later, we received the gift of going to the World Meeting of Families in Milan for a week! Recently, seven out of ten of us went with three hundred more and met up with millions in Cracow, Poland, from many nations of the world.

After commuting for five years, though, five hundred miles a week, with an hour and a half bicycle ride each way, various illnesses, a bladder operation, being knocked off my bike by a car, the work environment changed and I saw an opportunity to leave and to go into the deep (cf. Lk 5: 4) as a writer. Having acquired a wonderful range of experience as an administrator, editor, lecturer and course director, publishing various long cherished works and finally a book, I left with the project of another book coming together for possible publication. The book project turned into a trilogy and, together with various essays, has made concrete the "daily write" of being a writer.

After an anniversary Mass in the local Catholic Church, with older children now in the process of a work placement and university, my wife and I have just celebrated the miracle of twenty years of married life with a cappuccino with chocolate powder and a latte coffee!

Pointing back and pointing ahead: a Word of Life

Even earlier than the pilgrimage to Loreto, was the pilgrimage to Denver, Colorado, in 1995. It was as one in a million people on the plain, as it were, that I heard a word in the Gospel read by St. John Paul II: "I come to give you life and to the full (cf. Jn 10: 10); and, as it transpires, that word of life has triumphed down the years and, like a deepening grace, it is a word which has gone on being fulfilled throughout these years. The word of life, then, is a word which continues to unfold and, like the light itself, has many colours; but also, like the rainbow, bears the possibility of pointing throughout the remaining years to eternity and the final plunge into the fullness of life in the presence of God Almighty and the community of the angels and saints.

Part II: The Family on Pilgrimage

Introduction

In a more obvious sense this part of the chapter picks up the theme of the book as a whole; however, without the context of the rest of my life it can appear like an isolated event, almost idio-syncratic, when in fact pilgrimage had really begun to be an essential ingredient of our lives: as much "moments" of intense family life as "monuments" to providence transporting us out of our daily difficulties and routines. On the one hand there is nothing automatic about going on pilgrimage as a family; indeed, it brought to light how unprepared we were for travelling abroad. But, on the other hand, providence is nothing if not in the details of our lives and its events.

The "Gifts" of a Pilgrimage: "Una Famiglia" at the World Meeting of Families in Milan, 2012

More specifically, then, how was it possible for my wife and I and our eight children, aged between five and fifteen, to go to the World Meeting of Families in Milan?

It was a gift of Easter, 2012, to wake up and say: "Why not?" to the possibility of going to the World Meeting of Families in Milan. The main event was from May 30th to June 3rd, 2012, which implied all kinds of hidden costs. We had never been abroad as a family. Our family holidays were more about sharing with fifteen other members of my wife's family and the children playing, walking and swimming together rather than expensive outings or exotic destinations. With five out of ten passports, permissions to seek from two schools and the workplace, transport to organise, scarcely any surplus money and all the other problems of going was it even remotely possible? Abraham, I am sure, met a similar reaction from his wife when he said let us leave our country and our people and follow the voice of the Lord (cf. Ex 12: 1-9). How will we pay for it? Where will we stay? What about the safety of the children?

But the first person I asked to help with arranging tickets, as I had very little experience of travelling abroad, gave us £200 towards the cost. By the time we actually booked the flights we were able to fly from England at £25 per head and return, a week later, for £30 a head. I asked the organisers if we were able to stay a week with those giving us hospitality; and, although we could not go to where we were staying until the evening of the first day, they were able to put us up for the whole week. The children's schools accepted the educational value of the pilgrimage and we received the permissions we needed to go in term-time. The cost of the passports and photographs was a strain on our finances but we managed to complete the paperwork in time to go. As our car only has eight seats, we generally travelled to places with my mother-in-law bringing her car; but, in the early hours of Wednesday, May 30th, 2012, eight of us went by car and my wife and eldest daughter went by coach to the airport. Our flight was in the early morning and we arrived in Milan at about nine o'clock.

Milano: Una Famiglia?

By the time we had gathered ourselves we were the last people off the aeroplane and, together with our eight lots of hand luggage to keep the costs down, we passed the guardia as we left on our way out. One of the airport police called out what was to become a refrain throughout the whole visit to Milan: "Una famiglia?" ("Are you one family?") - as if it was a delightful surprise to see a larger family. There were young people at the airport to answer our questions and to help and so we decided to spend the day in Milan. By the time we had bussed it into the city, eaten our sandwiches, found some water and dragged our bags around we were getting hot and tired; but, fortunately, we discovered a large fountain on the edge of the city-centre and between the water, an ice-cream and a shady place to rest, we "weathered" the rest of the day until it was time to set off for our host family.

In view of the few days that we had before the main events of the pilgrimage, we took advantage of our surroundings and went for a walk and found a local park, ventured a little further and found a path beside a nearby river, visited a museum of stuffed animals in the centre of Milan and, at the insistence of our eldest, went on a visit to a prestigious shopping centre just off the Cathedral square. It was in the midst of a shop full of handbags that we discovered the enormously inflated prices of "labelled" crocodile handbags, especially when we knew someone who had worked abroad and had a clear idea of the cost price of these goods. At the same time we discovered that one of the big "labels" was willing to overlook the street vendors who were selling "fake" label handbags at vastly reduced prices; and, along with many others on the street, these people were trying to eek out a living.

The Papal Mass

There were numerous events which were a part of the pilgrimage "proper". There was the papal mass with Benedict XVI at Parco Bresso, at which we were part of an amazing gathering which, at the end, led off in a multi-stream of people in several directions; and, while anxiety for the safety of our children was generally present, it was then that I was most frustrated with helping our children to understand the risk of getting lost and the need to hold hands. My eldest son, with whom I remonstrated the most to hold the hand of one of his brothers, at first rebelled against my remonstrations and protested he would never go on pilgrimage with me again; but, more recently, when we were travelling to visit a university together, he not only looked back at Milan being one of the best pilgrimages he was ever on but he also did not even remember his outrage at my insistence that he help by holding the hands of one of his siblings.

At one point, we gathered for a common meal with all the other English pilgrims and their hosts; and, as a part of it, we were invited to give our experience of the whole event. I said that it was like St. Paul's experience of being a Christian: a Christian family was like being a spectacle (cf. 1 Cor 4: 9) - everybody could see the grace and human weakness. It was after our common lunch that we went for a walk around a nearby lake and one of our daughters kicked her trainer off into the water; and, even with a very long stick and various attempts, I could not recover it. Following a local practice, we fed the terrapins with dandelion leaves, and wound our way back to the main venue only to discover that everyone had left and that no English speaking people remained.

We set off in the hope of finding a way of getting back to our host family; and, after a while, we had to admit that we were lost. The children were getting tired and restless, pushing and shoving in the bus stop where we had stopped; and, to complete the picture, there was a nest of ants and all the fuss that a cry of ants engendered. On impulse, I insisted that we said one Hail Mary together; and, at the end of it, an elderly Italian man who recognised us from the common lunch earlier, stopped and got out of his car just as a bus drove up. He only spoke Italian but understood our plight. He persuaded the driver to let us all on for free and to drop us off at the bus station. Not only that, he followed the bus and made sure that we got on the correct bus at the bus station. Guardian angels do not have to speak the same language as us so long as they understand each other!

The Family on Pilgrimage

We returned from Milan with a number of memorable moments to share and, although we never managed to get to Philadelphia, in 2015, it is possible that we will manage to get to the next World Meeting of Families in Dublin, Ireland, on 22nd - 26th August, 2018[21]. I encourage you, therefore, whether it is the forthcoming World Meeting of Families in Ireland, the next World Youth Day, or another pilgrimage altogether, to consider going as a family. Who knows, at the end of the day, what contribution it will make to your family life, to your family history and to the experience of life that you will receive; and, in addition, who knows what difference it will make to others who saw you out of your depth, in another country, trusting in God, hoping in His help and finding it?!

Part III: The Life-Cycle Prose-Poems

Introduction to Chapter 1: Part III: The Life-Cycle Prose-Poems. These prose-poems are often a combination of particular and "synthesised" experience. The particular, direct experience,

---

[21] Cf. http://www.worldmeeting2018.ie/

being referred to roots the writing in a life lived: a lived life. But, even then, there is a kind of summary of lived experience, too, when seeking to show the way that paths are not always straight but repeat themselves, even if that repetition is also different; and, as such, that summary of lived experience employs the imagination in more obvious ways and, I hope, helps to show that living out of an unreal account of ourselves is like bubbling about as if the possibilities were more real than an undiscovered actuality. In other words, it is a part of this sequence of prose-poems that there is a gradual "de-bubbling" and a correspondingly seeping realism which, in its own way, does not alter the difficulties of life but helps us to see that there is a purpose which supersedes our own plans. Indeed, it may be that our own plans are what, possibly, give rise to so many problems. Thus, even if it is not without suffering, there is a "real" progress to be made in being a writer which, in a sense, is like the potential of the acorn seed: an inscrutably definite and real development that unfolds what is actually present.

In what follows each of the five Life-Cycle prose-poems is introduced by its title and a few words.

"The Life-Cycle Prose-Poems" were written out of a certain inability to communicate the struggle to identify who I am. Indeed, in a certain way, they are about giving a context to-coming-to-marriage: to the whole vocational account of being married which has entailed a sequence of pilgrimages and so many "words" which have illuminated who I really am and what is actually going on in my life. At the same time, however, these poems are about the almost inevitability of the "pilgrimage" nature of life; but there is, too, a kind of "fruitlessness" about these decades. On the one hand, it is true, there are many experiences to be written about; and, indeed, the temporal sequence, not always faithfully recalled, is also about going from possibility to possibility – but there is a kind of utter futility that arises from this deserted actuality. In other words, life-as-a-progression completely eluded me. On the other hand, then, these years stand as a kind of natural witness to the impenetrability of my own life: that it is as if there is in us that which takes a "word" to reveal; indeed, rather like "invisible ink" needed warmth or some other agent to make it visible on the page, so our lives need a "word of God" to make them truly visible.

These "Life-Cycle Prose-Poems", then, begin with what beginnings are recalled and what reflection suggests is significant; and, in time, wind their way through what, in living it, was often an interminable uncertainty about who I was: almost a terminal uncertainty in that suicide was not necessarily always going to be as unsuccessful as it had been. Thus these poems wash up, as it were, on the shore of a different kind of beginning and, along with being "grounded" out of the sea came the debris which, when pieced together, was in fact a number of precious moments or events which, not being deeply gathered, were dispersed and scarcely known. In reality, then, these poems are about a prolonged experience of "coming-to-myself" and, like the young man in the parable (Lk 15: 11-32), imply years of returning to the pigsty before finally being given the gift of hoping in God: 'God [who] could create everything out of nothing, [can] give spiritual life to sinners by creating a pure heart in them' (CCC, 298).

The Life-Cycle Prose-Poems

"Part A: Kaleidoscopic Changes" starts with an impression that our lives can seem overwhelmingly fragmented; and, as such, it is a matter of forming the fragments into "pictures" or "plans" and plotting, as best we can, a course for the future. The drawback, however, is that just as a turn of the kaleidoscope changes the configuration of the coloured bits and pieces, so does a change in life throw the combination of possibilities and plans into confusion; and, not knowing what a cycle of change was coming, I kept changing from one activity or work to another and never seemed any closer to the core of being myself – except that it was no longer possible to traverse the ground I had covered and, therefore, I was propelled to continue changing in the hope of ceasing to change again.

Part A: Kaleidoscopic Changes

I played football and wanted to be a footballer: bouncing a ball back and forth in a barn; climbing over the garden fence to play on the village green; and, even if occasionally playing in the village team, escaping the work my father wanted to do: escaping the relationship which would have helped both of us.

As I grew up I saw those around me choose courses and types of work, friendships and music, all of which left me wondering about where I had been while they were changing from children into "growing-ups".

Cards and walking home, having gambled away the bus-fare, were a tedious time-wasting substitute for living the maxim: know thyself. Going from school to college and from course to course signalled change without direction; and, going nowhere, I went where I was not ready to go: to the capital and to work. After table-tennis after work and solitary tennis against a wall, I started to read; and, at the same time as the lights, sounds and peopled discos beckoned, so did the multiplication of isolation in a floor of "others" prove an emotional impasse. I could not go in.

I left one job and tried another, even others, and started at Art School; and, although drawing established an objective, it raised the as-yet unanswerable question: what determines the choice of subject, training and work?

The "artist's" clothes were ill-fitting and fell off in the interview to go further. The ensuing confusion led back to the kaleidoscopic mirror of impressions and possibilities but nothing clearly distinctive, even singular, so much as another option and another interview, but this time an incomprehensible question about the mind and the body: as if the mind and the body were too distant to be intelligible and only vaguely indicated a "place" to visit - like a mountain to the man on the plain or "leaping" to a moon walk from jumping off a mound or swimming through the sea "translating" into a space-swim.

There were "transitional artists" from natural forms to abstract patterns, from whole objects to facets, from representational forms to those that shed their real colours and took on an array of moods and lights; and, similarly, the study of myself was somewhere in-between where I was and where I wanted to be. But the way forward was as unclear as ever except that the study of Shakespeare offered immeasurable delights of multiple meanings that expanded the horizon of questions to include good and evil and the multiplicity of nuanced arguments between a play as a whole and the "parts" and characters "acting out" aspects of a dialogue.

Short essays were impossible and did not "fit" the exam system of short answers.

Sociology, too, offered a possibility of thinking through philosophical ideas that were as different and varied as pieces of disparate puzzles; nobody, it seemed, knew the "whole" from which they came and one author after another had a bit that made sense amidst, as it were, a muddling of thoughts which never really got beyond being fragments.

I worked as a cleaner and lived in a room and ate and kept warm, occasionally losing myself in a read, not knowing whether I was at work or in the streets of Dostoyevsky's Crime and Punishment; and, embarrassed about my poverty, I would not often share the fire that needed fueling with money nor sit with others eating plenty.

Psychological problems suggested psychological answers; and, somehow, I ended up working as a psychiatric nurse, which opened a new range of questions about the body and the psychological expression of human suffering.

A young man explained that it was as if he was buried in a pyramid; and, knowing the intricate and misleading paths therein, he was expressing an "estrangement" from himself which was, in retrospect, not unlike my own. But, at the time, there seemed to be an impossible disunity in the study of human illness: an almost unintelligible emphasis on bodily processes being as meaningless as messaging tubes which, however, were almost never read, only intercepted or diverted. Or, conversely, there were those who studied the context of each human person and understood, in a way, how behaviour became more intelligible in the light of "local" relationships.

I lived in a room and shared facilities with others, encountered strange behaviour, got drunk accidentally on a lonely evening beside the bar, drinking cider like lemonade and falling over in the cold air and crawling back to my room.

Going on holiday was an experience with others in a mountain cottage, remote from even villages, where people behaved as if there was only one law: the law of acting according to a return to nature and "natural" substances.

But here I met a Shepherd who, for reasons of His own, was passing one night with a lamp which, briefly, offered hope and an anticipation of dawn, but which faded into incomprehension as the morning came and the day went on its way, unperturbed by the Stranger who, while He called in the night, went on His invisible way; and, as if the whole experience was "disconnected" from my life or the life of the Church, nothing made sense of it and I continued to wander from place to place, from person to person, from course to course.

Going to university to study psychology proved to be psychologically traumatic: studying fruit flies flew in the face of human meaning; and, even in the turn to philosophy, I encountered the whole bewildering weight of an almost undecipherable language and a new experience of isolation.

Christ "materialized" out of my upbringing and began to appear, again and again, in different guises: the "crucified one" speaking of forgiveness; the "crowned one", suffering in a silence difficult, if not beyond communication; the "complete man", to whom all good, true and human integrity points as to the perfection of all human identity.

Visiting different churches, discovering differences and, at the same time, obviously common characteristics although, in some cases, these were not a reason for seeking further fellowship as, almost, reasons for remaining apart.

A ship flew by through space and, in an arrow formation behind, all other boats afloat were trailing off to the left and right behind the flagship, piercing time and space and spearheading ecumenical progress.

Walking alone, I ended up in a psychiatric hospital and, after a while, following a visit from my father, I returned home.

■

"Part B of Kaleidoscopic Changes: Change" is, as it were, embodying that expression of a life lived in the flow: as if flowing from one activity or type of work to another was not just a waste of time but, in some unexpected way, was like the path of a particle through the universe. In other words, rejecting the everyday wisdom of completing the course of action chosen left me chasing, not infrequently, the change that would bring me just around the corner to a destination that I never managed to arrive at. But, trying and rejecting many paths, raised the intensity of the question: Is there a choice of work which expresses what we are more deeply than another or is it a kind of psychological illusion? Moreover, it is not as if the tide of human action does not run deep and, although running more deeply and subtly than we think, there are the thoughts that make it a necessity to wonder at the existence of conscience and wrong doing and the reasons which reveal the help to us of what is happening: a kind of feedback from our actual behaviour and a kind of cross examination on what it all means.

But then, too, there was the turning to prayer and the word from the Word of God addressing me, as it were, in such a way that I turned from what I was doing but did not see the way to go: a kind of goal blindness.

Part B of Kaleidoscopic Changes: Change

Change can be working with the hands as an expression of the practical intelligence: to build up a new beginning and to remedy a developmental deficit.

Going to and from the café for a winter tea, bacon butty and cigarette was beautiful!

But building was both an opportunity and an obstacle. An opportunity to do what I never did and to invent, paint, design, build and to enter that dialogue with material which turns in every kind of direction; but making things can be an obstacle, too, if it ends up as a kind of estrangement from the person I am: a kind of growing out of reach of where I want to be - without knowing where it is except that it is not being buttoned into building work.

Change can be going to the capital; but, instead of finding love, finding disappointment. The flowers bought and given deny, in the turning away from conscience, that the decision to be fleeting and brief is a "fraudulent gift": neither wholly given nor wholly received; and, all too soon, the splattering of brilliance and brightness washes away in the anxious wondering about being another's "experience" and, like the browning of an opened apple, the rot brings, at first almost imperceptibly, the colour of betrayal.

Changes, like ingredients undergo, are irreversible and un-reversible; but, at the same time, to take the broken egg and to make a meal takes a cook: an author of change beyond the range of messy bits. Just as wood cannot carve itself into a beautiful shape, nor stone assemble on stone, neither can we put the yoke back in the sac and, together with the white, return the whole back to the shell.

Wearily worrying about the choice of good or evil, the smell of "damned" despair or the enveloping layers of an eternally blooming "love-rose", "image" the contrasting possibilities of actions with eternal consequences.

Change can be a "success story" of earning money, acquiring tools and transport, driving miles and miles and working hours and hours, into the night, on my own, endlessly worrying about "work" running out; and, indeed, change can be about taking time to make a new piece of furniture: a design that "grows out" of the client's interests and plants, like the object it is, in a favourite place.

Working alone, in a place quiet enough to notice the leaves on a tree and the din made by a bird thrashing a snail against the ground, time is almost too slow to notice, full of pauses and wonderings about the point of it all: a kind of impossibly detailed moment in which almost nothing happens but colours and sounds and little movements expressing the presence of the universe.

Change can be a commission, to work inside instead of outside, with wallpaper instead of cement, bringing a man to life whose loss of legs had settled an unnatural silence in his heart; and, coming out of the house in a wheelchair, "walking" the countryside and smoking for a while in the fresh air, helped to find words-afresh on his lips.

Changes can be "totemesque", like the various faces on a tall pole, aspects of a life or two, juxtaposed; but too fixed, in a way, from one plane to another, whereas reality is more fluid - like the faces in a stream of "rubbling" water: bubbling as it runs and pours around the stones in the bed.

Change has moments like beads on a prayer chain; and, put together, they imply a whole design. But if there is no thread, no inkling of what went on from one "moment" to the next, then these "glazed" moments remain like unplanted seeds and, if they sprout, idly kick out shoots here and there but, unthreaded, are almost unprofitable to the grower.

Change, however, could be like cleaning which restores the originality of the gift; or pruning, which strengthens the plant; or being grafted, which brings what cannot be bought or obtained for ourselves; and, in a certain sense, change is all of these changes but, like growth itself, life entails a change unlike other changes: as if coming to exist is a paradigm of change.

Driving north, south, east and west, doing maintenance work, earning money, alone and praying; but, in the full flow of it, wondering what it was all worth and leaving it all behind.

Change can be unexpected and unpredictable, like the words of Scripture ticking across the horizon: What does it profit a man if he gains the whole world and loses his own soul? (cf. Mk 8: 36).

■

"Part C of Kaleidoscopic Changes: Bubbling Changes" is about those changes that seemed so important at the time and so inconsequential in later years; indeed, given my preoccupation with self-expression, the irony of it all is that the self that was expressed was so superficial. Driven by a kind of purism about only doing what permitted the permutations of individualistic choices, I scarcely made progress in acquiring a living; but, finally, the exhausting frustrations of failing to make progress began to turn me, more and more, to the possibility of guidance getting me to where I did not even know I wanted to go.

But even as good as guidance is, it cannot invent the self-knowledge necessary to making life-decisions; and, in a certain way, it is even possible to "assume" the mantle of a vocation without a real appreciation of its reality as "gift" and ordination to God. Thus it becomes evident how ill-equipped I was without the word of God: without an enlightening word that does not seek to flatter or to deny – but rather brings about that realism becoming to the human being as a creature.

Part C of Kaleidoscopic Changes: Bubbling Changes

What event came before or after another is difficult to remember; indeed, remembering what happened is like recalling "bubbles": a variety of moments in a multitudinous impression of erupting water, two or more sticking and clumping together, almost mixing and then there is calm again.

Memories, rising and bursting, being weighed and rejected, summarised or somehow flattening out into an impression of a time past; and then, "popping" the sense of a sequence and slipping around, as it were, until the meaning shines and, like a little rainbow, leads elsewhere.

Shapes arose, however, and seemed to fit various artistic possibilities: design; fine art work; and writing had been there too. But writing had been pre-screen and, unlike those who know and write, this writer had abandoned un-correctable pages of heavily glued changes, tippexed and unfinishable thoughts and reflections.

Working on a building site on the banks of the Thames one bright summer's evening and then going into St. Paul's Cathedral, the spirit flew as if unfettered: as if the very heart took flight in the fantastic opening that "visited" the visitor on entering.

I once went to a Church in Shropshire and stayed with the priest: replanting roses, praying and wondering what to do with my life; and, while I was there, I prayed for hours in what seemed like a "silent" Church: Who was listening?

I worked with a blacksmith: rubbing stainless steel shapes for gates, shaping bits of metal and considering the possibility of being a sculptor. Making a low and slightly curved garden wall out of old bricks and sitting on them in the first tea-break of the day, while wondering at the Canadian poppies which had opened in the warmth of the morning.

Carelessly I lifted too much and staggered, opening a recurring problem with my back which has only recently subsided.

Building a wall also took me to a remote village in Oxfordshire, where it was about repairing what had collapsed in the grounds of a retreat centre; and, occasionally, sitting in silence with the word and, much more frequently, daily working in the silence of outside noises and meals mostly on my own.

Going to London became living in London, this time with an "adopted" grandmother who cooked and helped with prayers; and, visiting a monk, I continued to work locally and to visit him periodically: making bread and visiting scenes in the bible was like "passing through" a passage of Scripture in which different ideas arose and, as such, swelled in pointing to St. Peter and the Church.

Otherwise I worked on a long shelf, prayed, met a woman I liked and almost led a "normal" existence; but, she said, she could not have children and, somehow, like slippery soap, there faded the possibility of continuing in each other's company.

I worked in a parish and was "clothed" in a certain "garment" through the possibility of a vocation to the priesthood: as if the very idea had robed me in a mysterious right to sacred things. There was work to do and I did it, together with others, praying and working on a variety of projects. But no bishop recognised any signs of vocation, although a local convent fed me very well and let me lead the prayers. People I helped came and went and those I visited went on with their lives after I had left, although the ambiguity of my life seemed to leave evidence in the expectation that I might return to marry someone.

An inner-city parish followed, at some point, with many people calling for sandwiches and life-story telling and, like a person that comes out from a crowd and goes back again, so many lives passed through and never would I know what happened to them.

Following the advice of the monk's Abbot took me northward again, further this time, to a religious order serving the destitute. But, in a storm, I left there and returned through the length of a rosary, to London and, in the end, travelling did what it had not done until now, turned me to a time of stability.

■

"Part D of Kaleidoscopic Changes: Changing Again" takes us into the turmoil of beginning to find change an inadequate response to life; indeed, as the years were passing and I seemed no closer to myself, the swirl of questions included doubt about the whole activity: but where to go if not to go on? Thus change, as it were, had the characteristic of an unbidden road too long to travel alone; indeed, like one of those desert roads, appearing to go endlessly on – but to where? How is it possible to carry on walking? Who knows how many people's prayers, beginning with those of my parents, were the reasons that I never gave up?

Part D of Kaleidoscopic Changes: Changing Again

We take what we think we know about ourselves and post a job application, turn up for an interview and even start work and, for a while, we enter into the tasks, day by day; but, gradually, the crises of life return and, like an echo, help us rediscover that in fact we have not found the place of rest: the place beside the stream where we scoop the water up and, as it slows and settles, we start to see, if we do not go on shaking it, the reflection of the person I am.

So I moved again, more reluctantly this time, thinking about the moss that I had not gathered and the seat that I had not sat in long enough to see anything beyond the swirls and changes, stress and struggles of surviving yet another change and its changes.

Like a washed-up bit of timber from a storm battered ship, still deluded about being whole, I was thrown out of the sea on a particularly strong wave and landed in a bed-sit, seeking to train to be a teacher of design and craftsmanship; but, in reality, pictures of ourselves, however formed, are false if not founded on a wellspring that we do not have to manufacture.

Making and drawing, however well done and evidenced in the living trail of actual work, carving and interior design, when turned into training and teaching, fell apart and dried up, yet again, another opportunity to progress beyond a few actualities and many possibilities.

From somewhere grew music, maybe from the few times that I and another had echoed in the subways, he playing guitar and I singing; or, alternatively, it was from those lonely years on the tractor, singing out in the countryside, prayers and variations on prayers; or, alternatively, those few times in a choir, scarcely managing to sing along with others. But then again, when others sing, almost like a song being sown as others sing, there arises such a swelling sound which searches, all the while, for a few words to voice and tremble, if possible, the unsteady steps to vocalizing what is within.

But no amount of practising improvisation on a saxophone in the snowy underpasses, recorder, guitar, piano scales or occasional songs, written and played on a few simple chords, music theory and lessons and reading about the history of music could transform a slight thread of talent into qualifying for a music degree; and, in one of those breathtakingly beautiful disappointments, I walked away from the failure to obtain a place at university with that freedom from fantasy which is such a gift of bursting bubbles.

So began again the search for a subject to study: mathematics, already a completely real "u" dashed any hope of medicine; leaving philosophy, law, psychology and fine art - each, in its own way, either making good a passage in the past or seeking, however clumsily, to open a fresh opportunity.

Languages came and went unsuccessfully even if, through perseverance, a few phrases or features of the variety of expressions would survive the difficulties of learning them.

And then, like choosing the last stone on the plain, there was a spring that sprang to life and came, both from the past and the pressing present: the question of life's meaning and the study of religion; indeed, it had arisen out of a candlelit memory of a school discussion which had, in contrast to almost everything else, succeeded in opening a chink in the hidden self.

Thus growing words again, writing again, for the course and then the courses for which they were written, started a new decision: to write the length required and to resist the writing of more than that; indeed, almost immediately, the more swilled out elsewhere and started off pieces of prose and poetry which, in one way or another, began to find occasional "frames" in one publication or another.

But, like so many other starts and stops, writing was amidst the on-going work of everyday life of shopping, health cures, cycling, visiting friends and questioning the existence of almost everything, paying the rent, finding work and, then, was it yet another bubble to be blown on the wind and disappear, again, after being rediscovered, again?

■

"Part E of Kaleidoscopic Changes: Or I Can Dream in the Writing" is about that return to writing via the needs of college courses and with the benefit of critical feedback.

Part E of Kaleidoscopic Changes: Or I Can Dream in the Writing of the Writer I Want To Be

Or can I dream in the writing of the writer I want to be?

But already there is bubbling up what has been forgotten and, indeed, when and where it happened, but happen it did: travelling from the north to the south, collecting a girlfriend and driving to London in time for the closing of the zoo! I remember freezing in a van, in the snow, awaiting something or about to go somewhere. There were times, too, of walking, alone, through the cities, towns and villages and only steps away from the doorways with blankets and a bowl.

So how can being a writer change all this?

What about those that have not made it and fell, who knows in what way and with what burden breaking them down, under trains or into rivers or in other, sad beyond describing ways of leaving families and friends and countless people on Facebook with a message scarcely understandable until it is too late?

How can writing make a difference to all this?

The challenge of telling how it is, "life", year after impossible year, of trudging through places and people's lives, on beaches and in the wilderness where only the lonely go and yet, time and again, going back into the Church and out again, wondering what it is about and why, anyway, go into a place that intensifies the isolation of being a-lone-er?

But God comes again and again and answers, differently each time, the questions in the heart and burdening mind until, finally, there is a moment of being beneath the waves and time, it seems, has paused as the light seems to be further away and then, suddenly, His help is understood, at last: to hope in He who helps those of us beyond the help of others who tried, even so, and did not understand the dying in the heart that trapped us in "tramping" times.

So what word upon word, written over many years, can bring another to kneel, not just at the rail as if it is a barrier but because it supports the weak and frail who come to pray at the empty crib - not because there is no Christmas Christ but because the emptiness is all the years told in the telling until a time started to turn into words what was happening in a way that telling told all the more the help we need: the beggar begging at the door of grace, broken, embracing the legs of Him who helps at the falling on the floor of those of us who failed, countlessly, to find a place to be the person we were until, almost too late, writing came to start again the life almost un-lived.

Oh do not give up; do not go into that dark place never to return; do not stop the search but search the search and discover, when all the questioning has ceased, that there is a "you", just as there is a "me", and that we must find a way to express what cannot be told except by you and me; because, somewhere, in whatever room or bridge or precipice, there is one waiting for a word: tell it to them so that they, too, may find a way forward to the life that is still to be led and, even after many tears are shed, is still to be lived and loved and, told in the telling, that others may yet live the life that "gifted" is.

■

In the first experience which follows, there is a very clear relationship between a life-situation, the "beauty of place" and the awareness of God, prayer and the vocation to marriage. There is, too, mention of the help of the religious and priestly vocations. Then there is another account of pilgrimage by a widow who looks back over her 81 years of life and how pilgrimage has been a part of it. Again, as in the first account, we see how one vocation helps another.

Alan Soares

My name is Alan Soares and I am 52 years old. I was born in Kenya, of Goan parents and emigrated to England with my family in 1972 at the age of 7. I grew up in a Catholic family, in east London, but moved to Cheltenham after getting married. I have been married for 22 years to my wife Daniela and we have six children. I am self-employed and volunteer at Cheltenham General Hospital and the local Sue Ryder Hospice, as part of the spiritual care team.

When I was asked by Francis to write a short experience on the theme of pilgrimage, I began to reflect on what an important role it has played in my history and my own spiritual journey.

Alan Soares: Pilgrimage and a Dialogue with God Leading to the Vocation to Marriage

My first real experience of pilgrimage was as a young man of 17 when I was on a family holiday in Portugal. We decided to make a one-day pilgrimage to the shrine of Our Lady in Fatima. I remember being left a bit cold by the huge basilica and vast concrete concourse. What really spoke to me was the winding coach journey up to the shrine and back. I could picture those young children in the simple beauty of the countryside and woods there, and it was this that made the apparition of the Mother of God much more tangible and real for me than the vast buildings.

This theme of sensing the presence of God in nature continued for me in my next taste of pilgrimage. I had joined a local youth club in my parish which was run by an Irish nun named Sister Julia. She took a group of us young Catholics to Galway, in the west of Ireland. Blest with glorious sunshine for our whole week's stay, we travelled one day to Croagh Patrick in County Mayo. Climbing this holy mountain, as saint Patrick had done, was for us an act of pilgrimage. As we climbed higher and higher, I began to realise why people throughout history and in the bible had built places of worship on high places. Delighted by the glistening streams of crystal water that gently flowed down the mountain side, I had a real sense of the divine in the beauty of the lush green grass at my feet and pearlescent blue sky above me. Towards the top the ascent got really steep and there was a real choice to be made as to whether to risk progressing or not. Encouraged by others who had gone ahead, and keen to help those wavering near me, I finally was elated to reach the summit. The panoramic views lifted my soul and my prayer of gratitude for having seen such wonderful sights came easily. The fact that we had travelled and experienced it together meant so much. Again this theme of Christian community and encouragement in pilgrimage would be one that would reoccur often in my life.

The next pilgrimage I made was when I was at college in Nottingham. I had been struggling on a degree course that I hated but didn't have the courage to tell either my parents or tutors as I felt I would be letting them down. Falling into what I now see as a depression, I virtually 'lived' at the chaplaincy, trying to find a meaning to my life there. One day we were visited by a charismatic young man named Ewan, who came from the Iona Community. Spellbound by his enthusiasm, a few of us from the Catholic Society decided to visit. Once again, the rare beauty of this gem of an island off the west coast of Scotland really struck me. I could see very well why St. Columba had chosen to found his little community there all those centuries ago. I found this type of Celtic spirituality very appealing, especially the way the monks used the nature around them to catechise people. Sitting one night on the small hill where St Columba built his cell, I was awestruck to see a huge golden moon rising out of the bay. For me, I heard the whisper of God's voice in the lapping of the waves and His healing touch in the caress of the gentle breeze. I could understand why Christ himself often sought out a 'lonely place' in order to pray and be alone with His Father. Another fruit of this pilgrimage was my first real experience of ecumenism, finding joy in praying, singing and having fun with Christians of other denominations. This desire for unity has stayed with me ever since.

By the age of 24 I had hit rock bottom in my life. I had failed my degree, was a slave to secret sins and was unemployed, spending most of my nights watching tv and most of my days sleeping. It was then that I finally gave in to the persistence of a faithful friend who kept inviting me to a catechesis to begin the Neo-catechumenal Way, one of the new movements in the Catholic Church. Here I heard a word of life and my life began to change. Just a few months before I had joined a community at St Charles Borromeo Church in central London, they had been to a pilgrimage to Santiago in Spain, meeting the Holy Father Pope John Paul there for World Youth Day. People who had gone couldn't stop talking about it; so by the time the next pilgrimage to Czestochowa in Poland came round in 1991, I was determined to go. This would turn out to be the most important pilgrimage of my life. At that time the 'cross' of loneliness bore heavily upon me. I had never had a girlfriend and my desire for a relationship and love had become a real 'idol'. I remember walking down Oxford Street one day a few months before this vocational pilgrimage and seeing what seemed to be beautiful girls from every continent pass me by. Each one who passed without even knowing I was alive was like a slap in the face and a dagger to my heart. After a while of this anguish I remember stopping and crying out to God. In that moment I finally accepted that if it was His will that I was to be unmarried so be it. Little did I know that in that moment I had in a metaphorical way raised my hand against the 'Isaac' in my life, as

Abraham had done. Within months, on the first day of the pilgrimage, I caught sight of a beautiful girl doing the liturgical dance around the reordered altar at Guardian Angels Church in Mile End, London. As God would have it, this girl would turn out to be my first girlfriend, and a few years later, my wife. Another highlight of this pilgrimage was to see literally thousands of people kneeling at the shrine waiting in prayerful silence to receive Holy Communion. At the vigil before the meeting with the Pope, tens of thousands of people were up, playing guitars, talking quietly etc. I was stopped in my tracks to see a Polish family of father, mother, son and daughter standing together with their eyes closed and praying the rosary with an incredible reverence - totally lost in the grace of the moment. It is a memory that has been burned into my brain.

Two years later I went to the next World Youth day in Denver, Colorado. My abiding memory of this pilgrimage (apart from courting my wonderful fiancée!) was the time I spent with Fr Alan Fudge, the parish priest of St Charles Borromeo, next to whom I sat on the coach for much of the time. This holy man has been one of the greatest influences of my life, and was truly like a second father to me. He was, without doubt, the most amazing preacher I have ever heard, never failing to announce the love and mercy of God for sinners like me. What struck me most on this pilgrimage was his sense of fun, and the countless times he made me laugh - that being a Christian is a joy and not all 'serious'.

The pilgrimage our community made at the end of the itinerary of the Neocatechumenal Way was to the Holy Land in 2013. This was for me a taste of heaven. To walk in the footsteps of the Lord, where he was born, where he preached, where he spent time with his friends, and where he died and rose again, was incredible. The welcome we received at the Domus Galilae, situated on the Mount of Beatitudes, brought tears to my eyes. To renew our baptismal promises at the River Jordan, at the probable site Christ was baptised, was a wonderful experience, and to have our three month old daughter baptised there was truly memorable. It was an incredible experience of communion with the brothers, of deep peace and joy, and above all closeness to the Lord.

Looking back I see how the Lord has used pilgrimage to move me when I have been stuck in a physical and spiritual rut - to be dynamic and not static, just as He is, to reveal Himself to me and put new hope and new heart in me, to connect me with others and to give me communion. My life has been incalculably richer for all this.

Clare Hill

I am an 81 year old who was widowed 15 years ago. My husband Frank and I had five children and fourteen grandchildren. My husband worked for GCHQ and I trained as a nurse and later in life, when the family had grown up, I worked as a Staff Nurse in a local Catholic Nursing Home, Nazareth House.

Clare Hill: Pilgrimage throughout 81 Years of Life and The Teams of Our Lady

I have experienced various types of pilgrimage throughout my 81 years of life and feel very privileged to have been a part of them. The first was in 1953 when I went on a school trip to Lourdes.

What struck me most, having never been abroad before, was the unbelievable length of time the train took to get there, about 24 hours, and the magic of seeing the Pyrenees looking like clouds in the distance.

I have been with my husband to Lourdes and Compostela, but the one that really stands out is Fatima. These were organised by 'The Teams of Our Lady', of which we were members. 'The Teams of Our Lady' is a movement for married couples to help them deepen their love of God and each other in their vocation to marriage.

On arrival at Fatima we were put into a Team of about 6 English speaking couples from around the globe. Everyone had their own group for prayerful studying of Scripture and sharing. There were many hundreds there from around the world as Teams exist in over 90 countries; so we met many other couples at meals or out and about. Different language groups wore different coloured scarves to help to identify them. Each day started with a wonderfully sung Mass concelebrated by the vast number of priest chaplains who had come; their procession to the altar was a wonderful sight to see. The sacred area around the Basilica is huge: Each day a different continent organised the Mass and hymns and people in their national costumes took up the Offertory in procession.

I have also been to Rome and the Holy Land with the Neocatechumenal Way. This was very different, but also a very wonderful experience. We were a community of about 50 people who all knew each other well and our guides who took us around the various sites connected with Jesus were very knowledgeable and helpful. Again we had Mass and times for prayer and sharing.

Chapter Two

In Pilgrimage to the Coming of the Word

General Introduction: The Coming of the Word

In the three parts of this chapter there are almost three steps towards the Word's coming.

In the first step there is the occasional poem, written at different times, in the course of my theological studies. At the same time, however, I recall that although I had begun the study of theology, it did not follow that a conversion of heart or an understanding of faith was at the root of it; indeed, this time entailed, as at other times, falling into sin and seeking confession: a kind of faltering following of Christ which, in reality, implied the power of human weakness to be powerfully present and active. In retrospect, it is clearer now than it was then, that the call to conversion can be relatively shallow: a growing recognition of the reasons for beginning to hate the weakness of the flesh; but, at the same time, a certain powerlessness in the face of it indicating a deeply addictive attraction to sin. There was a certain devotion-alism, too, almost a tangible consciousness of the presence of

Christ in the Eucharist. But, like a free electron out of the orbit of the nucleus, I was unable to fight off the attraction to sin – the unwrapping of the gift not completely given being stronger than the repulsing remembrance of the agonies which followed. Nevertheless, in the midst of this time, there emerged a growing attraction to the Church if for no other reason than the teachings of the Church, particularly of the popes, began to appeal to me: how well structured they were; brief, incisive and yet comprehensive accounts of reality; and, either explicitly or implicitly, expressing and raising real and challenging questions.

The second step, charted in Part II, brings out the more radical conversion to Christ through the moment of rejection: a rejection by Christ. I remember, in other words, as I began to see the good qualities of the Church in a rather impersonal way, such as the growth of small communities and a new emphasis on the Word of God, so I entered more fully into a superficial relationship to the Church: a kind of rational attraction to the goodness of it while, at the same time, resisting the recognition of being a sinner. Thus there came a point when, finally, I found myself in the Gospel of the wedding feast – as the man thrown out as he had not come in a wedding garment (cf. Mt 22: 1-14 [esp. 11-14]); and, in a newly radical way, I experienced the whole event of sin as a real wretchedness that led to contemplating suicide – to which Christ came with a word of hope from the *Catechism of the Catholic Church*.

The third and final step of this chapter is a reflection that looks at the diverse gifts of pilgrimage; indeed, pilgrimage implies but does not state so explicitly, that there is an almost involuntary witness to the help of God. In other words, given the many difficulties encountered in the course of fundraising, travel and accommodation, a pilgrimage is a concrete witness to us, and therefore through us, to the providential help of God. At the same time, however, the help of God is present throughout life and needs an occasion to make it more visible; and, therefore, it is about proclaiming the deeds of God as well as experiencing them in a variety of ways.

Thus this chapter has three parts. Part I: Three Poems: Our Mother of the Incarnation; Bread of Love, Wine of Glory; and Christmas; Part II: A Prose account of the Enlightening Work of the Word of God; and Part III: The Gifts of Pilgrimage.

Part I: Three Poems: Our Mother of the Incarnation; Bread of Love, Wine of Glory; and Christmas

Introduction to Chapter 2: Part I: Three Poems. In some ways these earlier poems are very focused on the summary nature of words and images; and, in addition, on the task of using a few words to express, intensely, the theme depicted. In a certain way, then, perhaps this is particularly appropriate to religious writing in that, very often if not of its nature, the Scripture draws frequently on real events and the imagery that arises out of them; and, therefore, perhaps it is a part of the natural impulse of human understanding to gravitate from the known to the less known: from the literal to the spiritual meaning of our experience.

"Our Mother of the Incarnation"[22] speaks, almost as dramatically as the wood itself, about the passage of suffering: that it enters and passes through us, as it were, in a very radical way; indeed, although the sculpture is static in comparison to our lives, perhaps there is, nevertheless, a sense in which pain opens a wound in our heart which never completely closes. The pain of redemptive loss, so amply expressed in the mystery of the crucifixion opening upon the resurrection, is a pain once experienced that never completely passes; indeed, perhaps it is one of the very redemptive gifts of pain, that the heart is enlarged

[22] "Our Mother of the Incarnation" was printed on the back cover of the September 1995 issue of *The Sower*. This poem was my response to the figure of Mary in *The Pieta*, by Fenwick Lawson. Mrs Dorothy Lee, Visitor Press Officer, York Minster, obtained for me both the picture and sculptor's permission for it to accompany my poem. Some small alterations have been made in this edition of the poem.

in a way that it cannot relinquish: that to relinquish the growth of the heart through suffering is actually to reject the increase of love it brought about. Although, then, this poem is not about the loss of a child through abortion, it does nevertheless express the unforgettable effect of it: that suffering the unnatural death of a child is a passage through unrepeatable pain to the hope of the resurrection.

Our Mother of the Incarnation

Mary's
split face
was carved out of a tree trunk.

Her sorrow
a shake in the timber
it had pulled apart:

a piercing-splicing
of wood and sky.

The grain did not split right down
nor did the heart come completely away.

What was opened
had not closed.

What began in the being of the Most High,
was hidden in the growing-green tree

is now open in the wound that Mary is unwilling to close.
And the sculptor
did not hide in her appearance:

he held in his hands
our Mother's grief
and wrought in his work
an opening to speak,

of Christ, our incarnation,
in His, our Mother's affliction.

Looking, I listened to
our Mother of the Incarnation
in the word-ripening-silence broken in wood,
to the ear-opening heart-making Yes in His our Spirit:

'Heaven opened in me a way down to man;
and man entered, in me, the way to Heaven'.

"Bread of Love, Wine of Glory"[23] was no doubt influenced in the struggle for words by Gerard Manley Hopkins, even if only slightly; and, at the same time, by the theme of marriage in the mystery of the Blessed Trinity and salvation history. On the one hand, there is no doubt that there are difficulties with "working back" from our experience, even our religious experience, to the mystery of God. But, on the other hand, the very concrete nature

[23] Published in *Second Spring*, Issue One, 2001, p. 20: secondspring.co.uk.

of bread and wine, wrought through its transformation in the history of salvation and the sacramental nature of Christ's action, is evidence itself of the intimate participation of the whole of creation and human activity in the work of God. Nevertheless, although salvation is a work of God it is, as it were, a work of love for us; and, therefore, this poem depicts that transfigured suffering which is the paradigm of God's gift to us.

Bread of Love, Wine of Glory

The Firebird
consumes to God
Christ's asphyxiation.

The Son's
threshed-pressed
separating soul
arose like incense
off His Body's cracked
Blood and Water.

Christ-risen
for our forgiveness,
carries back to man

the Dovetailed sign
of the cross
on dry land.

In the marriage
of that fledgling monument
God made man, of Himself a meal:

Bride and Groom
open Their lips
in fertile prayer;

and the Father's Breath
settles like a kiss
on our gifts.

The Mother in God
broods over the
fruits of His earth

and their being is born into the
Body and Blood of our Lord Jesus Christ:
Bread of Love, Wine of Glory,

Food for Their open-mouthed children
Drink for our thirsting through the desert
sign in our sudden flocking

and feathers to the heart
of man in flight
to the Most High.

"Christmas". At the time of writing "Christmas" I was staying in

London and attending a vocational discernment weekend; indeed, as far as I could see, I was there to become a priest or, at least, to determine if I had the vocation to be one. I had stood up on a pilgrimage to Denver, Colorado, to offer myself to the priesthood; and, as I recall, I almost avoided all contact with others as if "people" were contagious: a kind of "proximity" problem. At the same time, however, a woman on that pilgrimage had been wondering if I was a possible husband when, in her view, I stood up to offer myself to the priesthood and, simultaneously, severed the possibility she was considering. Nevertheless, as time went on, the possibility of the priesthood suffered a complete withering and this woman became my wife.

At the time of writing this poem, then, I was still in the process of discerning whether or not to go forward to the priesthood. I remember waking in the night and, unable to go back to sleep, writing down these first few words about Christmas. In retrospect, I am inclined to think that this poem sums up the excruciatingly slow progress of being transformed by the word of God into a Christian.

Christmas

I could not sleep
for dreaming
of when Christ
was made the fountain-head
of the well within the world
of God's grace;

and out-poured
a milk-white
lake of peace
in the midst of dead water.

On the inside edge of Heaven
wild beasts
drank themselves tame

Part II: A Prose Account of the Enlightening Work of the Word of God

Introduction to Chapter 2: Part II: The Coming of the Word. This piece was written in the season of Advent and, as such, brings to light the seasons of the Church which take us, as it were, through the life-cycle of the Church: the liturgically lived life-cycle of Christ. Thus this work was begun in the season of Lent which, according to some, reveals the Lenten characteristic of life as a whole: the unbidden but "free" penance of difficulties and illness. But we hope, too, in the voluntary acts which grace has prompted for the good of all. Thus this is a time to pray for fatherhood: to seek the graces of changing with the changes of our children and seeking to be that help to growing up which God gives us to be. Thus it is a time to turn again towards the prayer and persuasiveness to which I am unceasingly called.

Clearly, however, there cannot be a coming of the Word which is not, more completely, a coming of the Word of Life: an anticipation, even if remotely, of the Word of the Resurrection. In other words, even if it is a slow process, the process of the coming of the Word is multifaceted and neglects nothing: neither the good to be done here nor preparing us for the good of eternal life; and, at the same time, just as we exist as beings-in-relationship[24], then the coming of the Word to us is inseparably the coming of the Word to others.

In view of Advent: "The Word" in Words of Our Own: A Personal Reflection

Advent is a time of "coming"; and, what is coming but the Word within the word? What expectation, then, brings us to this Christmas? What birth of the word is possible in the busyness of our lives? What barrenness needs the blooming of a word beyond our words?

Scripture, according to the Second Vatican Council's, Dei Verbum, is a unique word: 'the words of God, expressed in the words of men, are in every way like human language, just as the Word of the eternal Father, when he took on himself the flesh of human weakness, became like men' (13). This is not, however, an account of this wonderfully scriptural, ecumenically sensitive, profoundly moving document which encourages us to meet The Word in the word; rather, just as "Ignorance of the Scriptures is ignorance of Christ" (St. Jerome, Dei Verbum, 25), ignorance of

---

[24] For a personal, philosophical and theological exploration of this theme see: *The Human Person: A Bioethical Word* (St. Louis: En Route Books and Media, 2017): http://enroutebooksandmedia.com/bioethicalword/. There are eight contri-buting Forewords from a variety of other writers. Or it is on Kindle for $9.99.

Christ is ignorance of ourselves (cf. *Gaudium et Spes*, 22). Therefore I have chosen "three words" and their graces, to write about in my own words. Although, however, there is a moment in which a word of God speaks to us, it can nevertheless takes years for its meaning to unfold; indeed, it is possible that because it is the word of God, it will never fully exhaust itself - but it will go on like light to the shores of eternity. Nevertheless, a word of God seeks, as it were, a hearing and, therefore, these are words which arise out of its "gentle impact" and express, however imperfectly, the life-print that indelibly arises from a meeting which leaves us changing if not changed.

The three words to be written about are: “The Wonder of the Word” never opened (I) "The Word that Came While Driving to London" (II); and the Cross in my History (III).

“The Wonder of the Word” Never Opened (I)

As a school boy I was distracted with gambling, stealing and fantasy comics about war. I remember burying a collection of pennies on a wasteland, carefully marking it with a heap of stones and then, to my utter dismay, being unable to find it amongst all the heaps that were actually there. But, even so, when I recall my childhood, there is present in it, nevertheless, a reverence for the word of God; indeed, I seem to see the Holy Bible on a lectern, ready to be read – but I cannot ever remember reading it. In other words, in a mysterious way, without knowing why, I was given a reverence for the word of God without ever opening it. It is likely, however, that I did read it in the school chapel; but, as I say, I do not remember being told that the Holy Bible was an unusual book or anything else about it.

I also remember, like a candle, in an otherwise frustrating and painful encounter with education, the rise of a question. We were discussing who could baptise and, almost for the first time in my life, I can remember being interested in the question posed. When, many years later, after many attempts at studying and earning a living came to nothing, it was this memory of being interested in a question to do with baptism that determined me "to try" the study of theology and, in time, philosophy, that have since become abiding pursuits.

This reverence for the word of God, however, remained with me for nearly thirty years without ever awakening in me a desire to open it; indeed, as it will become apparent, I read all kinds of books and, later, when I eventually started studying theology, I found it both very difficult to understand and a challenge to human understanding that this word was 'the word of God, expressed in the words of men'[25].

The Word that Came while Driving to London (II)

On the one hand, there were the failures: a failed attempt to get beyond an art college foundation year; to do philosophy or to complete a university degree in psychology. I was confused by the

---

[25] Cf. *Scripture: A Unique Word* (http://www.hprweb.com/2012/01/scripture-is-a-unique-word/). Later I brought together a book, drawing on all kinds of Scriptural investigations, philosophical and theological, as well as drawing on the Hebrew and interacting with embryological insights on the beginning of the human person; it took its title from the short essay and was also called: *Scripture: A Unique Word* (Newcastle upon Tyne: Cambridge Scholars Publishing, 2014).

question of my identity as an artist: Was I following in my father's footsteps; and, why anyway, did it matter if I was? As regards philosophy, beginning with the "mind-body problem" took me too far too quickly and, like one in front of an abyss, I retreated. The psychology, however, brought out my dissatisfaction with an analysis of human being which neither began with our actual reality and its depths and dimensions nor made sense of my own crises, possibly because I was too estranged from the everyday world of studying for a purpose beyond the agonising questions which beset and upset me, unrelentingly, driving me into every kind of quandary and its challenges. Into this situation of work and travel, came a word of God as I was driving to London. At some point, having trashed the attempts I made to become an artist, to be a writer or some kind of scientist, I had by now abandoned university and was beginning to be successful as a self-employed maintenance man, craftsman and interior designer. On the other hand, the "price" was an almost impossible schedule of hours into the night, weekends, long distances, local projects and an interminable procession of new places and people, except for those who began to advertise my work and help. I still had the workshop in the grounds of my parent's house where the silence was so clear that I could hear the "noise" of a bird breaking the shell of a snail on the side of a concrete car-pit. Not to mention the endless dreams and struggles to innovate in wood or to make sense of the wondering about the individuality of the leaves in the trees of the garden. Work seemed like a constant struggle to keep going when buying new tools brought no enduring satisfaction and simply added to the "weight of work" in the boot of the car.

Into this drive, in front of an amazingly wide sweep of landscape and sky, came the words: "For what does it profit a man to gain the whole world and forfeit his life?" (Mk 8: 36). I do not even remember looking this verse up in the Bible but I do remember going to London in search of spiritual direction and ending up with another five years of painful wanderings from religious life in Scotland to a Catholic Parish Worker, from Quaker Retreat Centre to an Anglican site for alternative medicine and, eventually, to a return to education and a time of stability. The Zen saying, "scoop up a bowl of water and wait until it settles", spoke to me of a much needed period of stability. After the failure of one attempt at stability another one, as it were, fell into place: a city and all its opportunities for further study - allowed me yet more failures at training to teach, testing out a musical talent and, eventually, the discovery of theology.

The Cross in my History (III)

By now I had begun to attend a renewal movement and, with rare insight, I understood that the difficulties which had beset me as a child and the disruption which had devastated my life were like the inside and the outside of a disease. In other words, I began to see that the many ways that I had misbehaved as a child was evidence of a hidden cancer which, as I grew up, showed itself in the devastation of my life; and, whereas I was normally and morbidly resentful of my life going nowhere, I began to see that the mess was like the symptoms of an underlying disorder which, while untreated, would continue to break out in life-problems.

This insight, however, while it made sense and gave me a certain amount of hope, was inadequate and a bit like a rational diagnosis of an illness that was beyond the reach of reason; and, in time, I found myself in the Gospel of the man thrown out of the wedding feast (cf. Mt 22: 11-14). In other words, I had “returned” to the Catholic Church on the basis of a renewal movement that enjoined a number of good practices on us: a collaborative ministry between a married couple and a priest; recourse to the word of God; and the founding of small communities. I left this way of formation and discovered, in an intensely painful way, that the reality I had glimpsed was not a psychological illness, even if it had in a way been present in my development; rather, the abiding and profoundly relevant discovery that I was still to make was that I was a sinner in need of a saviour.

One dreadful day, in front of yet another failure to live a chaste courtship and all the agonizing problems which are an integral part of that experience, I was ready for suicide; but, in the unfathomable mercy of God, in that very moment, through the very *Catechism of the Catholic Church* that I had begun to study, God came to my aid. As I travelled across the countryside, to and from the priest who was helping me to study theology, the fact of nature and its magnificent splendour stirred in me; and, in a moment too real but not too soon, I read the words of the Catechism which begot faith in me for the first time: ‘Since God could create everything out of nothing, he can also, through the Holy Spirit, give spiritual life to sinners by creating a pure heart in them’ (CCC, 298). In other words, the insight that I had completely lacked was not only my own sinfulness but the greatness of God’s help.

This Advent, then, I implore you to expect the coming of the word of God and the help you need, just as He gives this poor man the help he still needs (cf. Ps 34: 6).

Part III: The Gifts of Pilgrimage

Introduction to Chapter 2: Part III: the Gifts of Pilgrimage. It is possible to think of pilgrimages, and indeed our lives as a whole, in terms of our own efforts, plans and accomplishments; but, in the very nature of a pilgrimage there emerges the grace of gift: of really how the mercy of God has acted in our lives in countless ways. In a particular sense, then, pilgrimages are about witness: witnessing to a different mentality - to what we have been given and to what we want others to receive.

The "Gifts" of Pilgrimage

We can tend to think of pilgrimages in terms of costs, inconvenience and a challenge to our usual routines; indeed, we can even think that they are for other people: Are not pilgrimages for the saints, the sick or those on World Youth Days? If my parents could not go on retreat together with four small children, how was it possible for my wife and I and our eight children to go to the World Meeting of Families in Milan? How can we afford it? Why, anyway, bother with a pilgrimage? Indeed, mention pilgrimage in a conversation to an otherwise devout Catholic and you might get the following response: "When are you going on holiday?"

Why follow Pope Benedict XVI around England by car, indeed two cars, when we cannot afford the £1000 to travel on the coach or to go the shorter route with those travelling to one or two events? I can remember my wife complaining that it seemed "over the top" in comparison to just going on the shorter coach trip; but then, at one of the shrines we visited, her prayer to enjoy the pilgrimage was answered. Was it worth the long drive through the beautifully sweeping, sunlit mountains of the North of England; indeed, was it worth the weariness and the grumpiness which disappointed expectations revealed to be at work? What about the wonderful hospitality to our family, the parishes that helped us with food and the occasional gift of petrol money?

St. Augustine and the Catechism: A Word on Pilgrimage

So what, at a glance, are the "gifts of a pilgrimage"? To begin with a pilgrimage defines the Christian life: St. Augustine, a fourth century Bishop of Hippo and a father of the Church, says: "the Church progresses on her pilgrimage amidst this world's persecutions and God's consolations" (*Catechism of the Catholic Church* [CCC], 769). But a pilgrimage does not excuse us from the demands and development of this life; as it says in *Gaudium et Spes*, in the Constitution of the Second Vatican Council on the Church in the Modern World: 'Far from diminishing our concern to develop this earth, the expectancy of a new earth should spur us on, for it is here that the body of a new human family grows, foreshadowing in some way the age which is to come' (39). Thus we do not leave our lives behind but focus them on the essential needs of today and eternity: helping our children to see God act in our lives; indeed, our testimony is then taken up into their experience through the pilgrimages we have shared.

Pilgrimage and Easter

Even in the very origin of a pilgrimage, then, there is an inspiration to leave the "ordinariness" of life. It was a gift of Easter to wake up and say: "Why not?" to the possibility of going to the World Meeting of Families in Milan. Abraham, I am sure, met a similar reaction from his wife when he said let us leave our country and our people and follow the voice of the Lord (cf. Ex 12: 1-9): a reaction about all the difficulties to be encountered and had they been thought through by this old man who was, he claimed, listening to God. But the first person I asked to help with arranging tickets gave us £200 towards the cost.

Certainly not everything went well. When we visited the Basilica in which St. Augustine was baptised by St. Ambrose, we were too late to see the font and we were one among the million or more there for the mass with Pope Benedict XVI: and, indeed, it was a stressful experience shepherding our eight young children so that we did not miss the pilgrims we were with or the connections that we needed to make. Nevertheless, it was a landmark event of actually being a part of the World Meeting of Families in Milan; and, if reactions to us were anything to go by, then it confirmed the wisdom of Cardinal Angelo Scola hosting this event and witnessing, at the same time, to the life of marriage and the family. We shared, in other words, in this Cardinal's gift to Italian society.

Pilgrimage and the Holy Family

In another pilgrimage, my wife and I went with others but

without the children, to traverse the Holy Land. At a certain moment, as we swung around and down the Jordan valley in our coach, it struck me how slow and hot it would have been for the Holy Family to get about. By contrast, then, with our coach travel, the whole "reality-image" of the Holy Family and, later, Christ and His disciples travelling on foot, by donkey or by boat, remains in my memory like an answer and an encouragement in the face of the slow progress that I make as a husband, father and writer. In other words, there is a "walking pace" that reflects, more realistically, the "pace of God": a pace that addresses my life as a whole and does not, as it were, get me anywhere sooner than I need to be. Certainly I have wanted to complete courses, end unemployment, make more money more quickly; however, looking at life from the vantage point of sixty, what good did impatience accomplish?

Pilgrimage and Prayer

Later, on that same pilgrimage, we were in Jerusalem and an advertised walk through the way of the cross was cancelled, owing to unrest; but, for some inexplicable reason, our particular group was allowed to pass through the narrow streets with a cross and to stop and pray at various moments. I will never forget the grace of being given the cross and asked to walk with it and then pray, before passing it on to another pilgrim; and, in an unforgettable moment on the streets of Jerusalem, I prayed for the unity of Christians throughout the world: a prayer not excluding dialogue with anyone and everyone for the good of us all. There was also a wonderful opportunity to pray at the wailing wall and to receive a blessing from a rabbi and to witness, however briefly, the Jewish cherishing of the Torah as it was kissed in the course of being carried.

Pilgrimage and Going into Adulthood

Now, years later, seven out of ten of our family went to Cracow, in Poland, to meet with Pope Francis and hear the call to get off the sofa and to make a mark. The sign of raising £5,600 over and above our household expenses was already a gift and a witness to all of us. On the one hand it was an opportunity to share how the Lord had rebuilt my life and how indispensable His word is to understanding what He is doing in our lives: to bringing us out of an isolating "social media bubble" in which we risk the possibility of suicide through the starvation of real encounters in the reality of our lives. On the other hand, I was given the gift of giving a catechesis on Edith Stein which, while nearly passing me by because of the disrupted schedule of our pilgrimage, was eventually given at a Carmelite monastery in Czerna, Poland: as if from the intercession of the saint herself. What is more, on the penultimate page of her biography, I discovered that Edith Stein 'especially helps those searching for jobs'[26]. In other words, even at my time of life when I am setting out into the deep (cf. Lk 5: 4), pilgrimage is a word which brings encouragement, the call to faith and the comfort of heavenly patronage.

---

[26] *Edith Stein,* a biography by Sr. Teresia de Spiritu Sancto, ODC, translated by Cecily Hastings and Donald Nicholl (London: Sheed and Ward, 1952), p. 237.

Pilgrimage and the Fulfilment of a Word

The first time I went abroad was to Denver, Colorado, on a World Youth Day pilgrimage, it was to receive the Gospel proclaimed by St. John Paul II: I come to give you life and life to the full (cf. Jn 10: 10); and, although I had been unable to decide on a vocational path, complete any courses or develop lasting friendships, this word of life has been fulfilled over and over again. My wife-to-be was on this pilgrimage, too, but when she saw me offer myself for the priesthood, she dismissed further thoughts of me as a potential husband; however, as the events of life demonstrate, the Lord was preparing our hearts for a different vocation: the vocation to marriage and family life.

Finally, in the midst of the tragic and beautiful moments and places, the gifts of hardship and work, there remains the mixture of peoples gathered from across the world and the really colourful sign of millions of people on a few fields of earth: a reality-sign of the communion at the heart of God's gift of love to us. Thus the gifts of a pilgrimage are many and various and can last a life-time.

In the experience that follows, we see the relationship between pilgrimage and the vocation to the priesthood.

Dominic Quirke

My name is Dominic Quirke. I am 20 years old, born and raised in London. I am the third of ten children, from a Catholic family. I am a seminarian training for the priesthood for the Diocese of

Westminster, in a Redemptoris Mater Seminary. Having entered the seminary at 18, I am now in my third year of studies, studying theology.

Dominic Quirke: An Experience of Pilgrimage and a Relationship to God Leading to a Vocation to the Priesthood

When presented with the task of writing about my experience of pilgrimage, one thought came to mind: they have been a fundamental way in which God has worked with me in my life. They have occurred in a variety of settings, and in all manner of lengths and destinations, and yet what I realise in retrospect is that these details are to a certain extent insignificant. That is, insignificant in light of their primary purpose for me.

Personally, there is a common experience that underlies each pilgrimage, though they are different and occur in various contexts. God is always in a process of drawing me to himself, and yet I believe that pilgrimages are a moment of heightened opportunity and proximity, and have proved to be moments of great significance in my life as a Christian, even from a young age. What I have learnt is that by the mere act of movement, of coming out of a daily routine, and stepping away from the normal circumstances, be it out of choice or in obedience; there is a process of detachment and an explicit indication to be with God. That is not to say that I have always been entirely receptive in moments of pilgrimage, for this is not the case, but looking back they are milestones, important moments in which God has acted. I say this because my memories and experiences of pilgrimages highlight moments in which God has conferred certain graces and confirmed certain important decisions in my life.

I cannot pinpoint the exact moment in which I began to consider that God was calling me to be a priest. The fact that I accepted or even considered this calling was partly a fruit of my upbringing and education and the extent to which God had revealed himself to me then. However, it was only the beginning of a process; it was the first step in an explication. The unpacking and confirming of the verity of my calling was something that God would achieve through pilgrimages, these moments in which I had a greater sensitivity to what God's will was. Therefore, I recall going to Walsingham with my family at the age of eight or nine, and receiving a set of Walsingham rosary beads that I treasured, and at that point I developed a particular devotion to Mary. In the naivety and immaturity of a child of that age, my awareness of God's calling could only be manifest in a childlike desire, and yet even at that point my innocence allowed me to pray and it began a process, so to speak, of God revealing my vocation.

A few years later, as a 14-year-old I would go back to Walsingham, this time in the context of a vocational pilgrimage with young people from across England, in the Neo-Catechumenal Way. It was there that God orchestrated the first significant step in discovering my vocation. On the final day of this pilgrimage, there was a moment in which any young man who felt God was calling them to be a priest was given the opportunity to publicly express it by standing up, and receiving a blessing; not for show but as an outward declaration that one was willing to do God's will. I did so, and it was the first public expression I gave to the fact that I believed God was calling me to be a priest.

This began a process of many more pilgrimages, to Turin, Rio de Janeiro, Assisi, Fatima and Santiago, before I turned 18. Each of these pilgrimages were stepping stones. I'm not suggesting that pilgrimages are the only instance in which God speaks, by no means, and yet they were moments in which God confirmed in me first of all that he was calling me to be a priest, and secondly the grace that I was willing to reciprocate. They each contain many experiences and memories, all of which are important I believe to build towards one thing, which is my relationship with God. Several of the pilgrimages I mentioned were specifically vocational pilgrimages for boys considering the call to priesthood, in the context of the Neo-Catechumenal Way. We would go away for a week or so and spend the time together; it would be a time of sanctity, in which there were moments of prayer, of time with the Word of God, with the Eucharist each day, and also of just being together. We would visit historical sites and shrines, and learn about the Saints and listen to catecheses about vocation and calling; we would spend some days walking for miles in the countryside, together praying the rosary. In a sense, the descriptions exalt the pilgrimages beyond what they were, they sound deceptively pious, which they weren't. They were occasions on which very ordinary young men spent a time together under the guidance of a priest, who sought to lead them to God, who reveals his will.

This is ultimately the underlying experience I have had of pilgrimages: that I am given the means by which to come closer to God. God orchestrates and inaugurates this and the pilgrimage has been a crucial way in which he has done this with me. There have been moments in which by the Word of God, by catecheses, by the lives of the saints and prayer, God has slowly manifest his will to me and confirmed again and again. Just before I turned 18, I was on one such pilgrimage, to Santiago de Compostela, and it was the moment in which I had in front of me the decision to go to the seminary in the new academic year. Following the seven or eight days of pilgrimage that had preceded it, I made the decision, in a moment of clarity, of freedom from distractions and temptations, and in a time in which I had been with God and recognised again that it was His will. I cannot say what I would be doing or where I would be without the fruits of the pilgrimages I have been on; but what is for sure is that God has used them as a very important means by which to reveal his will to me and to give me the grace to follow Him.

This process did not come to an end upon entering the seminary, but is something that continues, and pilgrimages continue to be a moment in which God presents to me an opportunity to be close with Him, to distance myself from routine and distractions and present my life before Him and wait for Him to speak. For this, though I have had wonderful experiences visiting the various destinations that my pilgrimages have presented me with, I have come to recognise that the pilgrimage is an external sign of something God is calling me to live internally, to see His will and follow Him. My vocation is the fruit of all the pilgrimages I have gone on; however, at the centre of both my vocation and any pilgrimage, is for me to come to have a relationship with God.

Chapter Three

World Youth Day Pilgrimage, 2016

General Introduction to Chapter 3: A World Youth Day Pilgrimage. In a certain sense this pilgrimage began in an Anglican Abbey, although one older than the Reformation, in a chapel dedicated to Our Lady and, more than a year later, ended with a prayer of thanks in that same chapel. While on the first occasion there were the other pilgrims with whom we were fundraising and travelling, not even ourselves having decided to go yet, on the second occasion there were several from our family and the remembrance, on visiting this chapel again, that we had in fact been to Poland and back. Thus, as I recall the time we spent fundraising, traversing Europe and the visit with Pope Francis in Cracow, I am inclined to think that this pilgrimage was in fact a gift of Mary: even an ecumenical gift of Mary. A pilgrimage, then, is often about more than we realise; and, therefore, I am sure it was also about our relationship to Mary, Mother of the Lord and to Joseph, her spouse. In a certain sense, then, a pilgrimage is about our relationship to the whole Holy Family who are, I am sure, accompanying us in our pilgrimage through family life and all that makes it up: both the ordinary and the extraordinary events of life. Perhaps, too, in view of the growing rediscovery of the "mystery" of Mary, Mother of the Lord, perhaps the Holy Family is central to modern ecumenism.

But, more prosaically, even in the event of finding it difficult to fix a towel rail in the bathroom, having tried various styles, I have prayed to St. Joseph and then "invented" a construction which took advantage of the weak fixing and used hanging flower basket brackets and tubes between them to make a reasonably lasting place for some of the several towels to hang. More importantly, then, there are innumerable times that I have turned to St. Joseph to teach me how to be a helpful spouse and father. Likewise I remind the children of the childhood of Christ and, I am sure, of the generosity of His parents in looking after other people (cf. Mt 12: 47). Thus their family life informs our actual daily life in all kinds of ways.

Part I is about how and why we raised the money and went on pilgrimage with over three hundred others and around two and a half million more (I). The next two pieces give an overview of the pilgrimage to Cracow (II) and a more specific account of a reflection on Edith Stein, based on a catechesis which I gave, as "her gift to me", in a Carmelite Monastery in Czerna, Poland (III).

Part I: Raising Awareness and Money

Introduction to Chapter 3: Part I: Raising Awareness and Money. Why fundraise for 7 out of 10 of our family to go to Cracow, WYD, 2016? My wife and I had not been on a World Youth Day pilgrimage for a long time and never as husband and wife, not least because they were out of our reach financially. Two of our older children had managed to go on a number of these pilgrimages and, one way or another, they had managed to raise the money to go by packing food at a supermarket, doing odd jobs or various sponsorship activities. But this time it was going to be four of our eldest children, then five as we thought it would help the next one down and then seven as my wife and I decided to go. I was the one, however, who really wanted to go; but my wife, declaring that if God made it possible, said that she would come, too. God making it possible for us to go not only included raising the additional money but also finding families to care for the three children we were leaving behind: the three who alternately challenged our desire to go with their fears of what would happen to us or just wanting to be with us and to come too.

Poland is, after all, the homeland of the Pope whose work I have studied more than any other writer: St. John Paul II. Thus it seemed an opportunity too good to miss. Having discussed this with those overseeing the pilgrimage, it was suggested that my wife and I could go as a part of the team of catechists.

There are three sections to what follows: a brief note on fundraising for a pilgrimage (I) the challenge and mystery of fundraising itself (II); a reflection on St. John Paul II (III).

I: Fundraising for a Pilgrimage: Being a Pilgrim

In 1964, the Church called chapter seven of her Dogmatic Constitution on the Church, *Lumen Gentium*, "The Pilgrim Church". Thus the fathers of the Second Vatican Council spoke of 'some of his disciples ... [being] pilgrims on earth' (49). It is a "natural part", therefore, of the life of the Church to be a pilgrim; indeed, it might even be said that a Christian is a pilgrim: a person-in-pilgrimage: a person en route to eternal life: a being-in-relation who is called to cultivate his relationship to God and to his neighbour. In other words, it is not only that the pilgrimage has a value in the life of the pilgrim and indeed in the life of the Church – showing us very concretely our dependence on the providence of

God; but, in addition, it is a witness to those around us that this life points to eternal life – as it is also a witness that in the midst of this life's difficulties God helps us.

Fundraising for a pilgrimage, however, invites us to tell people what we are doing and, in that way, to raise awareness about the existence of these events and, in a small way, to give a witness about the work of God in our lives. At the same time, however, setting out on the whole process of fundraising is also a call to prayer: to pray through the many difficulties of useless fundraising projects, rejections and criticisms; and, in the end, it maybe that the value of all the difficulties, especially the criticisms, is precisely that it is a call to pray and to hope in the action of God.

II: The Challenge and Mystery of Fundraising for a Pilgrimage

Fundraising for a pilgrimage can be challenging. We are a family of ten and seven of us planned to go on the World Youth Day pilgrimage to Poland, this last Summer, without taking anything from the family budget. A few thought it was too much to fundraise for this pilgrimage for five children, aged eighteen down to fourteen, never mind for my wife and for me to go too! As upsetting as this was, we prayed.

As a part of our fundraising, I had written to various places, telling them what we were doing and £600 was the response; indeed, it was not as if I knew the people personally but, nevertheless, they responded to the request. One small company I visited asked me to write to them and they paid £100 into the pilgrimage account. Most of our fundraising, however, was the selling of cakes and the ridiculous generosity of people who obviously wanted the whole event to succeed. One Saturday we did a "Cake and Candles" sale at one of our local Mass Centres, and not only raised nearly two hundred pounds but received the promise of another £500! Wishing to impress this donor with an aspect of our itinerary, I told her about the salt mines in Poland in which a cathedral had been dug out of the rock – only to discover that this particular person had not only been there but had taken her disabled daughter too!

Our fundraising took 11 months, beginning with a sponsored walk and a prayer in Tewkesbury Abbey's Mary Chapel; and, following my wife's insistence, we waited until the children were paid for until we started taking more than the initial deposit for our own costs. We ended our fundraising with a written appeal to a variety of people as we were still short of £1,307 and already a week over the deadline for the final payments; and, would you believe, an Abbott wrote back and apologised for his delay in responding and asked what we needed. I replied that we needed £1,307 and, using the pilgrim payment website, the Abbott wrote off the whole outstanding sum. Altogether, with the older two children doing some part-time work, we raised £5,600 to go to Cracow; and, therefore, the Lord made it possible for us to go without spending our household income.

Concretely, we understand very well the difficulties of being a large family and, at the same time, how the providential love of God shows itself in many ways. I have, for example, five higher education qualifications and have been given invaluable experience, but also have been in receipt of poor wages and persecution in the work place. Thus I speak not out of bitterness but out of a realism faithful to the reality of life; and, what is more, the new opportunity of writing for a living is a providential gift: a new kind of setting out into 'the deep' (Lk 5: 4; cf. Lk 5: 1-11) – even in view of it being intensely difficult to earn anything from it! One of the unexpected gifts of the pilgrimage was to give a catechesis on Edith Stein who, it turns out, 'especially helps those searching for jobs'[27]; and, moreover, in that she was a writer who had experienced all kinds of work difficulties herself, I was encouraged to hope that she understood what I was doing and was a kind of personal advocate with the Lord.

III: The Inheritance of St. John Paul II

At the time of Pope St. John Paul II visit to England I was undecided about my Catholic inheritance. Indeed, if I went to Church at all, I am not sure what it was based on: a kind of habit; a vague sense of the presence of God; an admiration for the Word of God, although I never opened the Scripture; the possibility of meeting other people; a desire to be helpful? However, I remember looking at a televised picture of St. John Paul II and thinking: this is Peter. Although it was still to take a number of years, I eventually started reading the papal writings which, contrary to many claims, were both very readable and full of wisdom; indeed, these works were a particularly helpful

---

[27] *Edith Stein,* a biography by Sr. Teresia de Spiritu Sancto, ODC, translated by Cecily Hastings and Donald Nicholl (London: Sheed and Ward, 1952), p. 237. In Part III of this trilogy on the Cracow pilgrimage, which is more focused on Edith Stein, there are numerous citations from biographies, Edith's own autobiography and other works.

contribution to my intellectual formation and, furthermore, raised fascinating questions about the nature of the human person, being open to life and conception.

As I became aware, however, of what other people thought, it was clear that the truth that these documents so clearly taught was not self-evident to everyone and that, in so far as people tried to explain themselves, it seemed that the essential problem was that they thought that what the Church taught could not be lived. This, however, was a different question to the truth of the Church's teaching; and, in time, I discovered that I, too, could not live the beauty of the truth.

Although I have studied the works of Karol Wojtyla, John Paul II, for a number of years, I am not persuaded that the answer to the chasm between recognizing the truth and living it is simply about the extent to which the Church's teaching is advocated personalistically; indeed, the argument that a better presentation would have prevented the poor reception of *Humanae Vitae* has some merit[28] but overlooks two, if not three elements of the real situation. In the first place, the work, which entailed developing an adequate anthropological account of the human person is a profoundly deep and positive work, which continues today; indeed, it continues in precisely the direction espoused by Blessed Paul VI: Married 'love is above all fully human, a compound of sense and spirit' (9). Furthermore, 'Human intelligence discovers in the faculty of procreating life, the biological laws which involve human personality' (10); and, ultimately, there is an 'inseparable

[28] Cf. George Weigel, *Witness to Hope: The Biography of Pope John Paul II* (New York: HarperCollins Publishers, Inc., 1999), pp. 206-210.

connection, established by God, which man on his own initiative may not break, between the unitive significance and the procreative significance which are both inherent to the marriage act' (12). In other words, it is no small task to develop an adequate account of how human love is a 'compound of sense and spirit'. Indeed, the question of how human love is a 'compound of sense and spirit' goes to the very roots of human being (cf. 13), raising the question of the very origin of human personhood: that the human person is precisely a psychologically inscribed biological being. The unity of human acts follows, that is, manifests, the natural integrity of human being.

Secondly, then, the biography of St. John Paul II[29] shows how immensely immersed in the pastoral work of married people was the young Karol Wojtyla; and, in effect, how the pastoral principle of the priest's "accompaniment"[30] of married people is really a profound indication of the daily necessity of the presence of Christ in the life of the Christian.

Thirdly, then, what cannot be underestimated is the extent to which the religious man can live a faithless life: a life that does not actually express the reality of a living faith in Jesus Christ as a daily Saviour.

In conclusion, then, not only do we underestimate how profoundly challenging it is to think through the human condition, in all its wondrous simplicity and complexity but there is, too, the real need to live a living faith and not just practice a kind of proximity to the Church which, however helpful, leaves the

---

[29] Cf. Weigel, *Witness to Hope*.

[30] Weigel, *Witness to Hope*, p. 106.

conversion of the heart untouched. There is no doubt, then, that St. John Paul II has contributed immensely to my life and to the pastoral, philosophical and theological heritage of the Church. Just, then, as his biography is helping me to grasp the reality of his wonderfully integrated ministry, so I hope that going on pilgrimage to Poland will help me to deepen my perception of a son of Poland: a fruit of Poland's Faith. If, then, Poland has a sense of its mission in the world what, then, can it teach us about our mission in the world?

A Note on the Vocation of the Writer

What is the vocation of the writer? It is indeed to participate, widely, in the discussions of the day. The variety and depth of St. John Paul II's participation in the life of his country[31] is almost a template of contributing to the culture of a country - to the culture of the world[32]. Clearly, then, there is a sense in which the vocation of a writer is influenced by the great authors that have been read; and, indeed, by seeing in their lives that living expression of dialogue, life and word. Distinguishing, however, what pertains to the ministry of a priest, bishop and indeed pope, there still remains a variety of writing which, legitimately, a layperson can contribute to the life of a country and to the culture of the world; for, in many respects, although written work still originates from particular people in particular places, it is

---

[31] Cf. Weigel, *Witness to Hope*, pp. 211-215; however, there is no doubt that the biography, so far, is a marvellous witness to John Paul II's multifaceted contribution to the socio-cultural life of humanity.

[32] E.g. philosophy; poetry; plays; theology; catechesis; prayers; letters etc.

nevertheless true that its availability is more readily global than it was. This almost immediately transmissible material of the writer, then, brings with it the need to be almost scrupulously responsible in what he or she says; and, at the same time, it is surely to the point that the writer loses nothing of the necessary vitality, vividness and "voice" that makes the word-challenge so appealing, enthralling and potentially engaging.

In conclusion, then, the whole project of fundraising included revisiting the work of St. John Paul II through Weigel's biography and seeing it afresh, as it were, in the context of his life. In recalling the work of God in our lives and pilgrimage being an almost inseparable part of being a human being and a Christian, it is clear that God acts through both the positive and the negative aspects of even a good work. Finally, there is a kind of "multiplication of loaves" in the very sharing of everything that God has done; and, indeed, whatever good He does in our lives is almost increased as it is "distributed" to others (cf. Mt 14: 13-21).

Part II: Europe and a Conversation

Introduction to Chapter 3: Part II: World Youth Day, 2016, Cracow: An Event in the Faith of our Family. It became clear, then, as the possibility of our pilgrimage became increasingly likely, that even if the three younger ones were not coming, they were still involved in the call to faith which is an integral part of the work of a pilgrimage: faith that God exists and rewards those that seek Him (cf. Heb 11: 6). Thus our dialogue with our younger children was very much a part of our dialogue with God and almost a kind of "over-spilling" of the purpose of the pilgrimage into our whole family life. Thus, just as the fundraising had taken us on walks and to numerous cake sales, so the event and even the significance of the pilgrimage had deeply affected even the youngest members of our family; indeed, in a certain way, perhaps they had benefited the most although they had not actually come with us.

Similarly, however, it was noticeable that the pilgrims' real life experience which was shared, which was in a sense our inheritance from our conversion to Christ, was one of our most valuable possessions; and, time and again, it was recalling the different events of our history that was often a part of what was to benefit those coming through the early adult years of life.

At the same time there is no doubt that visiting places brings history to life as it is lived in the "today" (cf. Heb 3: 13) of the contemporary world.

In what follows there are a number of sections: Leaving our youngest children behind and an unexpected beginning (I); Highlights from the pilgrimage as a whole and a particular conversation (II); and Final impressions (III).

(I). Setting off and leaving the younger members of our family

Seven out of ten of our family went to the World Youth Day, in Europe and Poland from the 22nd of July to the 3rd August, 2016; indeed, without the many people who paid for cakes as if they were jewels or simply gave donations, we would not have gone on this pilgrimage. Just as the man in the Gospel says 'I am not strong enough to dig' (Lk 16: 3), so I am no longer strong enough to raise money through manual work. Writing, then, was my contribution to the fundraising, which entailed a vast number of emails and a few letters; in addition, however inadequately, writing contributed to the "evangelization" that is almost an inseparable part of the whole endeavour. Altogether this is a part of the mystery of the death and resurrection of Christ: the God-man who turns water into wine (cf. Jn 2: 1-11) and our sufferings into joys. The Good News is that God loves us, acts in our lives and made this pilgrimage possible. Thus I thank God for the two families, too, who looked after our three youngest children while we were away. It had been a very difficult time for our younger children as they had been filled with anxiety for months about our safety owing to the unpredictability of terrorism; and, in the end, we entrusted ourselves to the founder of the World Youth Day pilgrimages, St. John Paul II and, as their fears arose, so we encouraged them to turn to God in prayer as indeed we did ourselves.

Travelling to a Different Schedule

We left, then, around midday on Friday, 22nd July, without internet screen phones and with a car stuffed to the brim and roof box crammed with baggage, being driven to London to begin the pilgrimage with the sacrament of reconciliation with over three hundred other pilgrims. It was indeed wonderful to see so many queuing for confession. What is more, the exhortation that what was planned may well not happen was intended to help us enter into the expected difficulties of being a part of a world-wide movement of over two million people to Cracow. So, when we set off for Dover and found ourselves in a traffic queue, owing to an atrocity in France, stricter security checks and holiday makers heading for Europe, we remembered the words about possible changes to the schedule and boarded the ferry to France on Saturday evening instead of the early hours of Friday night.

Whatever our expectation of going to Amsterdam, owing to the long delays we had to pull over for the night and leave the first part of the itinerary to those who had made it across the ferry in good time. Owing to the need for driver breaks, at first the Polish coach drivers were going to park up and leave us for a comfortable bed; but then they changed their minds and drove to a lorry park and we all slept in the coaches for a second night. Having anticipated that my wife and I would be too old for the difficulties of the pilgrimage, I was delighted that we both managed to sleep and to bear with these and other minor inconveniences. Significantly, however, our young people found the opportunity to get to know each other an adequate compensation for the journey stalling so soon; and, what is more, we began the common prayers of the pilgrimage, morning prayer and the rosary, and we found that there was a good spirit among us in our difficulties. Our first Eucharist, then, instead of being in a convent in Amsterdam was on Sunday morning in a lorry park in Belgium. It was a beautiful morning and, by about nine o'clock, we celebrated the Eucharist on a picnic table suitably adorned with cloths and candlesticks.

It was almost a taste of the early Church: the word, the Eucharist, each other and the witness of a Eucharistic celebration in a lorry park amidst peaceful and beautiful countryside. It is a part of the legacy of St. John Paul II that the Eucharist was celebrated on mountains, on the site of the Church-to-be-built at Nowa Huta and in a variety of other places. We also knew that we had passed refugee camps in the night and that our hardships were temporary and nothing in comparison to what other people were going through. We drove all day Sunday and arrived an evening earlier than planned at the hotel which was to accommodate us on Monday night; it had been possible to book an additional night, as well as to buy ad hoc meals as we travelled. On arrival, we booked in, grateful to be able to wash and to get to bed.

(II). Highlights from the pilgrimage as a whole

It would take far too long to write and to read a detailed account of the pilgrimage to Cracow; and, in a sense, it would overlook that there are "natural" variations in the significance of what we experience. Thus, in what follows, I shall focus on those moments which come to the fore, for one reason or another, in view of the needs of the contours of an interior landscape which, streaming as it does, nevertheless leaves "places of stillness" amidst the plethora of detail and activity that is possible in even the quietest of days.

The Word of God

In the light of a recent suicide, I realise that it is possible to be "connected" to many people and, at the same time, to be unknown in the midst of them. Thus I had come to the pilgrimage intensely conscious of how important it is that we are enlightened about the reality of our lives; and, in my experience, the word of God, the Bible, is indispensable to this enlightening. It is not enough that we suffer, we must know the significance of our suffering; and, at the same time, it is not enough to suffer "naturally", we need the help of Christ to act in our life. Nor is it enough that we suffer on our own, we need the communion that the communication of suffering, enlightened by the word of God, helps to bring about. On the one hand, then, the word of God contains an immense wealth of human experience; and, on the other hand, it is possible for it to make explicit the hidden or incompletely conscious tendencies in our hearts. Thus the word of God is able to bring about fellowship in the reality of life and the relationships through which we are brought to salvation and the possibility of eternal life.

It is possible, then, to be well known and unknown; and, indeed, to be well connected and unable to communicate the depths of our hearts. Thus, as Pope Francis and others said at their meeting with us in Cracow, we need to make contact with each other, to get off the sofa and to come out of our isolation and build bridges, believing that God looks at what we can still become and the mark that it is still possible for us to make. Thus it was an important part of our pilgrimage for each person to encounter a word of God from a Gospel and to respond to it and, at the same time, to have the help of others to identity the richness of this word for each one of us. Thus our pilgrimage was "seasoned" not only with the prayer of the Church, the word of God and the Eucharist but with the shared experience of the reality of our lives.

In a visit to Katowice we met a few of the lay people who had contributed to the "mark" of a magnificent Church built under communism and then we viewed the film "Karol", based on the early life and ministry of St. John Paul II, which showed that the vocation to love opens up a new beginning in otherwise impossible situations of injustice. At the same time, social change was a part of what was brought about by the more general vocation to truth, the rise of Solidarity and the help it was to the development of Polish society; and, while not without its pain, there was both the fall of communism in Poland and, later, the dismantling of the Berlin Wall in Germany. We were then given a marvellously generous buffet dinner. Together with another witness from the Carmelite Monastery at Czerna, we saw how becoming a monk freed a man to be who he is; and, for many people, the words of the monk remained an encouragement not to be afraid to tell friends about their religious reality. We encountered, directly and indirectly, many ways in which people of all walks of life had left their mark on society.

A Conversation

I recall, too, an unplanned conversation with a Jewish woman and her husband. We had received a catechesis on the Christian roots and development of Europe, visited a Memorial to the Murdered Jews of Europe and set off towards the centre of Berlin, passing the remains of Checkpoint Charlie and the Berlin Wall, in order both to decide on a meeting point to determine our return to the coach and to go in small groups in search of lunch. My wife and I and our companions found an Italian cafe and, as I noticed a woman eating a large salad, I asked which one it was on the menu. I then went on to explain what we were doing and where we were going and the woman replied that they were Jewish, although non-practicing, and that their children were too young for them to visit Auschwitz. I also explained that the Second Vatican Council was a watershed in improving Catholic-Jewish relations and that, in particular, there was a recovery of the Passover as the foundation of the Catholic Eucharist or Mass; and, to my surprise, she said that we were very fortunate to have both the Old and the New Testament to complement each other.

In a brief exchange with her husband I said how helpful it had been to study the opening lines of Genesis in the original Hebrew as, unlike English, Hebrew was a grammatically gendered language; and, therefore, certain aspects of the opening chapter shone through in the Hebrew which are otherwise almost totally obscured in its translation into English. Thus, for example, the words for the 'heavens and the earth' are a pair: the first was grammatically masculine (shamayim [heavens]) and the second was grammatically feminine (aretz [earth]). In addition, there is the complex identity of God. Elohim: a masculine plural used in the singular; and, therefore, creation is understood to be a singular act of a "plural" God. Then there is the marvellous "feminine" expression of the Spirit of God. Ruach Elohim is made up of a feminine noun, Ruach, usually translated as Spirit, influencing the choice of a feminine participle, merahefet, over the masculine noun, Elohim, as in the expression 'the Spirit of God was moving over ... the waters' [Gn 1: 2]). Thus, although the 'Spirit of God' is almost colourless in English, in Hebrew it bears a distinctly complex gender: almost as if a "feminine" Spirit is proceeding from a "masculine" Godhead. When, later in the chapter, the author "announces" the creation of man, male and female, the Hebrew text makes us realise that he has actually prepared this announcement through the structure of the chapter up to that point.

However brief this conversation was, then, it was nevertheless a small but significant fruit of a growing, but truly holy rapprochement between Jews and Christians and, indeed, between Catholics and Jews. It was also a part of my own, more interior pilgrimage, as I was reading my way through various biographies of Edith Stein, a Jewish convert to Catholicism, and some extracts of her work. This was in preparation for a catechesis I was to give at the Carmelite Monastery in Czerna, Poland. Edith was born in 1891, on the Day of Atonement, a day of reconciliation between the Jewish people and God, and she died in 1942 at Auschwitz, gassed along with others in reprisal for a letter written by the Dutch Bishops denouncing anti-Semitism. Edith offered her life for both persecutors and persecuted. On the one hand, it is true that Edith Stein had requested a papal denunciation of anti-Semitism and the growing anti-Catholicism; and, at the same time, she had deplored the Government of the day's identification of itself as Christian. But, as I went round Auschwitz-Birkenau, I saw how brutal had been the reprisals if people had either escaped or resisted their captors. Thus I understood vividly the problem of inciting these reprisals. On the other hand, then, this helped me to appreciate the agony of prudence that belonged to public authorities in determining what action to take against anti-Semitism during the Second World War.

I took comfort, too, from the amazing number of people, from so many different countries, who had included Auschwitz on their itinerary during the World Youth Day pilgrimage; and, at the same time, who were passing through these places of pain so respectfully and, no doubt like us, were conscious of all the questions which arise in the human heart in front of it. Thus there is the hope that they too were striving to think through the evil in the heart of man and how it needs to be constantly recognized and addressed by the grace of God.

(III). Final Impressions

It is already evident that we have passed through many places, all with their history, their present, our impressions and encounters and the innumerable questions which arose within us and which we both shared with others and which we will no doubt go on thinking through in the years ahead of us. One of the words which was to remain with me were those of Sr. Faustina: 'Jesus, I trust in you'. Another word was that spoken by our chief catechist, Lorenzo, in the context of our evangelization and witness in the square at Wroclaw: Thank you for the persevering faith of the Polish people.

We saw many sights and heard many sounds, passing through many peoples' life and work, including an underground Cathedral in the Wieliczka Salt Mine, the Centres for Sr. Faustina and St. John Paul II, including all the varied architecture and interior artworks and exterior landscaping, Wroclaw, the birthplace of Edith Stein, St. Teresa Benedicta of the Cross, and the miles and miles of open countryside that ran between and within the various countries we traversed. In the St. John Paul II Centre there was a painting of him with the Mothers and Fathers of Poland: the celebrated saints of Polish history. While there, I was conscious of the desire of St. John Paul II to find married saints[33]; and, indeed, it would be fitting for there to be, one day, a Sanctuary of the Family, depicting holy husbands and wives, beginning with Adam and Eve, Abraham and Sarah, Joseph and Mary.

In terms of a lasting "image" of the pilgrimage, I am left with the impression of peoples from all over the world, coming together in the presence of the head of the Catholic Church, Pope Francis, who turns us to the mercy of God expressed in Jesus Christ and His Church. It is almost as if this were a "world breath". At the same time we were in receipt of many acts of kindness, from the student hostel's cafe owner and staff, our Polish drivers, the Polish authorities who both organised and assisted with the main religious meetings of the pilgrimage to the many local people who left their hoses out to cool down the pilgrims on their walk back to the coaches after praying with Pope Francis. Although we live in times in which there are many painful reasons which bring people to move, this movement of pilgrim people "from" innumerable countries of the world and "back" to innumerable countries of the world, is about people discovering a communion which has the possibility of being a "leaven" in the world: a leaven of hospitality and welcome in the reconciliation of peoples.

We are a part of an ongoing pilgrimage

Even very recently, in the dialogue between Pope Francis and

---

33 Cf. Weigel, *The End and the Beginning – Pope John Paul II*, p. 286: 'John Paul II fulfilled a long-standing ambition and celebrated history's first beatification of a married couple, Luigi and Maria Beltrame Quattrocchi, three of whose children were present for the Mass in St. Peter's Square.'

the Lutherans in Sweden, we hear of an understanding of our common faith that speaks to the roots of conversion: 'With the concept "by grace alone", ... [Luther] reminds us that God always takes the initiative, prior to any human response, even as he seeks to awaken that response'[34]. In other words, it is possible to make the pilgrimage of faith that finds unity in diversity; and, in the right spirit, to rediscover the reality of the Christian faith in communion with others. In a different context, to some '200 representatives of other religions – Christian, Jewish, Muslim, Buddhist, Hindu and others', Pope Francis said: 'Religions are called to this way of life, the Holy Father affirmed, "in order to be, particularly in our own day, messengers of peace and builders of communion, and to proclaim, in opposition to all those who sow conflict, division and intolerance, that ours is a time of fraternity"[35]. Finally, I read that a '30-member delegation of the Council of Religious Community Leaders in Israel met in Poland', visiting Auschwitz-Birkenau, and together they said: 'We repudiate racism, fanaticism and extremism, particularly when these are committed ... allegedly in the name of religion and in so doing desecrate religion'[36].

Thus I recall that our pilgrimage, so steeped in the Europe we traversed, is indeed a part of an immense and wider pilgrimage of

---

34 October 31st, 2016, Zenit staff, "Pope's Homily at Ecumenical Prayer Service at Lund", https://zenit.org/articles/popes-homily-at-ecumenical-prayer-service-in-lund/.

35 November 3rd, Kathleen McNaab, https://zenit.org/articles/pope-calls-all-religions-to-follow-path-of-mercy/.

36 November 4th, Paweł Rytel-Andrianik, https://zenit.org/articles/appeal-for-peace-from-auschwitz/.

the people of God: of all people who are seeking to be reconciled, to live in peaceful coexistence and to foster dialogue and common action for the good of all.

Part III: Feminism and Edith Stein

Introduction to Chapter 3: Part III: A Gift from Edith Stein (1891-1942): a Modern "Mother" of the Church[37]. Edith Stein was born into a Jewish family on the Feast of the Atonement, 1891, and died a Catholic Carmelite nun, St. Teresia Benedicta of the Cross, in Auschwitz in 1942; she is an 'eminent daughter of Israel and faithful daughter of the Church ... [and] a saint to the whole world' (2)[38].

There is a terrible temptation to look the other way, to pretend that we live in a different world or to believe that we are different to the people who lived and died in the atrocities of the Second World War. However, in reality, what we have seen is a spread of the mentality that rejects the gift of human personhood. On the one hand there are marvellous inventions which benefit us, whether it is increased international communication, motorised wheelchairs or personal computers. But, on the other hand, there is a disease that has spread: an uncritical, unaccountable and unrestricted belief in technological development; indeed, it is as if the new "sin" is the very possibility that sin exists: that there can

---

37 This has now been published by Fr. David Meconi: http://www.hprweb.com/2017/09/a-gift-from-edith-stein-1891-1942/.

38 Homily of John Paul II for the Canonization of Edith Stein, Sunday, 1998, https://w2.vatican.va/content/johnpaulii/en/homilies/1998/documents/hf_jp-ii_hom_11101998_stein.html.

be anything other than progress and endlessly exploitative innovation. The human conscience, paralysed under the influence of bureaucratic "distance", the ideological denial of a common humanity or the goal of a greater good for everyone except the people whose exploitation make it possible, needs reawakening. Edith Stein, then, is a witness to a feminism which develops the whole human race and is an antidote to the dying humanity which we daily witness.

There are the following three parts to this article: an account of the origin of this reflection in the World Youth Day pilgrimage to Cracow (I); the context of modern feminism (II); and, finally, a number of specific aspects of Edith Stein's life and work (III).

Edith Stein in the Context of the World Youth Day Pilgrimage to Cracow (I)

Ordinarily, I would never have read about a woman who had been gassed at Auschwitz. As a young student, having seen pictures taken by the allies who entered the concentration camps at the end of the Second World War, I had no desire to revisit this reality. However, over many years, it has become clear that the mentality that can reduce people to 'biologic' beings is still with us[39]; and, indeed, biologism is expressed in the mentality that

39 Cf. Evelyne Shuster, "Fifty Years Later: The Significance of the Nuremberg Code", New England Journal of Medicine, 1997; 337: 1436-1440: http://www.nejm.org/doi/full/10.1056/NEJM199711133372006 (Source Information: From the Veterans Affairs Medical Center, University and Woodland Ave., Philadelphia, PA 19104) at the end of this excerpt she cited the following reference, at footnote 12: 'Complete transcript of the Nuremberg Medical Trial:

considers itself biologically superior[40] to the point of determining the death of those defined as inferior. But the contradiction needs stating more boldly: Who, equally in receipt of the gift of life, has the right to take it from another?

The problem is, therefore, the problem of an inadequate account of the human person; indeed, biological identity is, in reality, a beginning which needs the complementary analysis that is open to the fullness to be investigated. The contradiction inherent in the intelligent explanation of human, "biological" being is beyond the power of ideologically driven exponents of biologism to appreciate. In other words, in elective abortion, in the stark reality of a child being torn from the womb, the perpetrators believe that this child is a 'biologic' reality – not a psychologically inscribed biological reality that begins the gift of human personhood. Even in view of the inconsistency of tearing out a boy or girl, there is the wealth of human reality which is expressed in the relationship of son or daughter, grandchild or niece or nephew; and, therefore, there is a wealth of human suffering that is brought about at the same time. The reality of bureaucratically programmed deaths, in other words, is still with us: the "processing" of the abortion of a human being suppresses the very humanity he or she has in common with the person whose gift of life has been stolen. The terrible irony remains: the abortionist has received the gift of human life which is taken from others.

United States v. Karl Brandt et al. (Case 1). Washington, D.C.: National Archives, November 21, 1946–August 20, 1947. (Microfilm publication no. M887.)'.

40 "Übermensch": 'The term Übermensch was used frequently by Hitler and the Nazi regime to describe their idea of a biologically superior Aryan or Germanic master race' (https://en.wikipedia.org/wiki/%C3%9Cbermensch).

However, visiting two memorials to the death of ideological racism has shown me that the mystery of this tragedy and the triumph of hope do need to be pondered upon and prayed about[41]. The first memorial was in Berlin, a deliberately bare set of giant shapes like tombstones, inscribed, in one place, with the stark words: Memorial to the Murdered Jews of Europe[42]. Whatever the controversies that surround this work, I could not but admire the blunt statement of truth which constantly calls consciences to be open to the reality of this human suffering: of all human suffering.

The "second memorial" was the camps, Auschwitz I and Auschwitz II-Birkenau. As we processed through these camps, thousands upon thousands of us, passing through on the way to the World Youth Day meeting with Pope Francis in Cracow, there was a reverence in the process of assembling, passes being checked and then winding our way through the various scenes and accounts which now identified what went on in the barbed, but extraordinary ordinariness of the buildings and their beautiful surroundings of trees and fields. What I did not expect to discover was hope, hope that expressed itself in the liberation of the camps and the raw witness to what went on and came to an end.

As I read about Edith Stein, what encouraged me was the attractiveness of her personality; indeed, a certain contrast between her patient, cheerful helpfulness in everyday life and in

---

41 During the World Youth Day pilgrimage to Cracow, 22nd July to 3rd August, 2016.

42 https://en.wikipedia.org/wiki/Memorial_to_the_Murdered_Jews_of_Europe

the extremity of awaiting execution[43] and my tendency to grumpiness, especially towards the end of the day.

It is a truism that nothing comes to exist but that it has a context in which it comes to exist; and, therefore, Edith Stein's life and work comes to exist in the context of a many-faceted "moment" in modern history. She is a woman who lived the love that completes the truth of nascent feminism, the need to recognise the right of all races legitimate self-expression and development, the need to integrate new philosophical insights with perennial truths, the need to improve Jewish-Christian relations[44] and the mystery of a lived "love of the enemy" (cf. Mt 5: 44)[45]. 'St Teresa Benedicta of the Cross says to us all: Do not accept anything as the truth if it lacks love. And do not accept anything as love which lacks truth! One without the other becomes a destructive lie' (6)[46].

---

43 Cf. Joanne Mosley, *Edith Stein: Woman of Prayer,* Leominster: Gracewing, 2004, p. 14, quoting from Posselt, Sister Teresia de Spiritu Sancto, *Edith Stein,* pp. 54-55.

44 Carmen Hernandez (1930-2016), the recently deceased co-founder of the Neocatechumenal Way, has likewise contributed significantly to the enrichment of a Catholic understanding of the Paschal Mystery through a life-long assimilation of a positive dialogue with Judaism. Moreover, many young women 'said it was thanks to Carmen they found pride in being a woman" (http://www.catholicherald.co.uk/news/2016/07/20/carmen-hernandez-co-founder-of-neocatechumenal-way-dies/). Carmen is, possibly, yet another Modern Mother of the Church.

45 Mosley, *Edith Stein,* p. 50: Edith's 'love went out to both the oppressed and the oppressors.'

46 Homily of John Paul II for the Canonization of Edith Stein, Sunday, 11 October, 1998.

Edith Stein in the Context of Modern Feminism (II) The Identification of Women in the Church

We are used to thinking in terms of the Fathers of the Church, profound Christian thinkers from the early part of the first millennium, and the Fathers of the Second Vatican Council (1962-1965). The Fathers of the Church were a wide variety of early Christian writers who reflected on almost every aspect of the Scriptures and the spiritual life. St. Augustine (354-430 AD), for example, is cited in the document of the Council on the Word of God, showing an early sensitivity to the implications of divine-human authorship: 'God speaks in Sacred Scripture through men in human fashion' (Dei Verbum, 12). In other words, it was precisely as 'true human authors' that God inspired the writers of Scripture (Dei Verbum, 11); and, therefore, God spoke to us through the very humanity of human authorship (cf. Lk 1: 1-4). Blessed John Henry Newman (1901-1890) was not actually present at the Council and yet influenced it in a number of ways, particularly in its reference to the lay vocation[47]: the vocation of being Christian, whether or not it is expressed more specifically in the vocation to marriage or the priesthood.

Edith Stein (1891-1942), then, later and younger than Newman, is no less an influence on the Council and the modern development of the Church. It was, after all, not until 1970 that Pope Paul VI made St. Teresa of Ávila (1515-1582)[48] the first

---

47 http://www.americancatholic.org/Features/Saints/saint.aspx?id=1946: 'Blessed John Henry Newman' (1801-1890).

48 Cf. Pope Benedict XVI, 2011:

woman Doctor of the Church: a Doctor of Prayer in a world too often too busy to pray[49]. As a part, then, of the general rapprochement concerning the overlooked contribution of women in the life of the Church, Edith Stein is one of three co-patronesses of Europe, along with three male patrons of Europe[50]. Thus I regard Edith Stein as a Mother of the Council and a Modern Mother of the Church.

At the same time, however, the very existence of female religious orders is itself a witness to the ongoing contribution to the development of the identity of women which, from the Old through to the New Testament, has been expressed in innumerable ways; and, as such, there is plenty of work to do in a reasonable account of the contribution of women and the positive, if not uncritical assessment, of the mystery of the Church to the identity of women throughout the centuries. Therefore I am not an avant-garde feminist. Indeed, in the words of Pope Francis, St. John Paul II answered that there is no possibility of a woman's ordination to the Catholic priesthood; and, explaining, he said: 'the Church is the Bride of Jesus Christ. It is a spousal mystery. And, in the light of this mystery one understands the reason for these two dimensions: the Petrine dimension, namely, episcopal, and the Marian dimension, with all that is the maternity of the

---

https://w2.vatican.va/content/benedict-xvi/en/audiences/2011/documents/hf_ben-xvi_aud_20110202.html

49 Cf. http://www.ctkcc.net/carmelite-corner/pope-paul-vi-on-st-teresa-of-jesus-as-doctor-of-the-church/

50 Cf. http://w2.vatican.va/content/john-paul-ii/en/motu_proprio/documents/hf_jp-ii_motu-proprio_01101999_co-patronesses-europe.html

Church, but in a more profound sense'[51]. In the mystery of salvation, then, the mystery of woman is an expression of the mystery of salvation: that God acts in us; and, in keeping with the iconography of this mystery, Christ chose the ministerial priesthood to be an expression of the vocation of a man[52]. But, nevertheless, there is a feminism which needs to be identified and developed[53]; and, therefore, Edith Stein was in the forefront of advancing the reasonable development of the identity of a woman.

A Real or an Imagined Injustice to Women?

In the case of the Catholic Church, then, it is widely "claimed" that denying the possibility of the priesthood to women is an injustice. If the priesthood of the Catholic Church is an expression of a specific ministry of Christ Himself, then it is clear that Christ chose men precisely for this purpose; indeed, as men, men were "created" in view of a priestly possibility that was never envisaged for women. Nevertheless, in view of our baptismal consecration as

---

[51] November 2nd, 2016, Pope Francis' Interview on Return from Sweden: https://zenit.org/articles/full-translation-popes-in-flight-press-conference-on-return-from-sweden/.

[52] In her article, "The pitfalls of a gendered theology of church", Natalia Imperatori-Lee, says: 'this complementarity [of masculine priesthood and feminine Church] also casts the laity in the Marian role and the clergy and hierarchy in the Petrine office. This is potentially problematic, as it rests on the passivity and submission of the "Marian" principle (the laity) to the Petrine (the clergy)' (http://www.americamagazine.org/content/all-things/its-not-complement). But the problem with Imperatori-Lee's point is that it overlooks the following: that it is the whole Church, expressing the mystery of mankind before God, "who" stands to God as feminine in virtue of the necessity that God acts in us for the sake of our salvation: 'apart from me you can do nothing' (Jn 15: 5).

[53] Cf. St. John Paul II, *Letter to Women*.

priests, prophets and kings, there is a priestly work of teaching which is a part of the vocation of women, as Edith says: 'The spreading of the faith, since it is included in the priestly vocation to teach, is predominantly the task of men, though women, too, are active in this sphere, especially in the teaching Orders'[54].

Where, however, is the injustice if men and women are constituted as dynamically different, complementary "expressions" of human personhood? What if, from the beginning, God expressed a radical difference in human personhood, precisely as a vocation to the mutual enrichment of both men and women; and, therefore, what is the radical benefit of womanhood and, indeed, of the contribution of specific women to the life of men, marriage and family, culture, society, the Church and the world? Why, in other words, is a ministry which is exclusively reserved to men not an injustice to women?[55] There is, in other words, a vocation in virtue of being a woman which is as indispensable as being a man but characteristically different. Perhaps it is a help, therefore, to reflect on this in the light of Edith

54 *Writings of Edith Stein*, selected, translated and introduced by Hilda Graef, London: Peter Owen Ltd., 1956: pp. 161-173, are an extract from "The Ethos of Women's Professions"; and, therefore, the quotation comes from p. 168 of this version.

55 There is clearly a ministry for women in that, as a woman Bishop of Gloucester, Rachel Treweek was by far the more able preacher at an event at Tewkesbury Abbey (2016): the conferring of various levels of the Bishop's Award in the Joint Anglican and Catholic Academy of All Saints. In the strict sense of being a Bishop, however, the ministry is "constitutionally" different in an Anglican communion to what it is in a Catholic communion. Nevertheless, as I say, Bishop Treweek spoke in a memorably attractive way about the Christian life and how it is lived. She said that the cross, for example, she wore around her neck was made of bits of war machinery: a fitting "modernization" of the cross of Christ transforming an instrument of torture into the vehicle of our salvation.

Stein, an early advocate of genuine feminism.

Edith Stein: the Person (III)

How do I Come to be Writing about Edith Stein?

Writing about Edith Stein, however briefly, is another aspect of the gifts I have been given through the 2016 World Youth Day pilgrimage to Poland. As a member of a team of catechists who went with more than three hundred young people to the World Youth Day meeting with Pope Francis, my wife and I attended a pre-pilgrimage meeting. A team of around twenty catechists were called to finalise the preparations for the pilgrimage, which included the possibility of giving a number of catecheses in the course of a nine day journey from London to Cracow; and, although I am much more familiar with the work of St. John Paul II, I was vaguely aware of a philosophical affinity between Karol Wojtyla and Edith Stein and, attracted by a slight familiarity with her connection with the late Pope, I offered to prepare a catechesis on Edith. Reading began and continued, both in the lead up to the pilgrimage and during it. As the schedule of the pilgrimage suffered from one delay or another it looked as if the opportunity to give this catechesis would slip through the changes in the timetable. In what I regard as a gift from Edith herself, I eventually gave the catechesis in a Carmelite Monastery in Poland[56].

[56] To over three hundred pilgrims at the Discalced Carmelite Monastery, Czerna 79, Czerna 32-065, Poland (Thursday, 28th July, 2016).

Edith Stein: Philosophy; Judaism and Feminism; Prayer and Self-offering

I began reading about Edith Stein and almost immediately fell in love with her reasonableness, her prayerful discovery of her vocation and the dialogue she had with her confessors, the obvious kinship between her philosophical and theological work and the papacy of St. John Paul II and the modern development of the Church's teaching on the complementarity of men and women, Jewish-Christian dialogue and the attractive goodness in how she did the good she did. In particular, then, although there is not an explicit reference to Edith Stein in the opening catecheses, in 1979, of St. John Paul II's Theology of the Body, it is possible to see the whole cycle as summarised in Edith's understanding of the opening chapters of Genesis. Edith says: 'We shall find in ... [the Word of God] ... the traces of the original order of creation, of the fall and of the redemption'[57]; and, in the words of St. John Paul II, we see that Christ appeals to the beginning and to the original order that 'has not lost its force, although man has lost his primeval innocence'[58]. On the one hand, then, it could be that both of them have been thinking with the Church[59] and understood, albeit in slightly different ways, the enduring reality

---

[57] P. 112 of the *Writings of Edith Stein,* selected, translated and introduced by Hilda Graef, pp. 101-125, "The Vocation of Man and Woman".

[58] John Paul II, *Man Woman He Created Them: A Theology of the Body*, Translation, Introduction, and Index by Michael Waldstein, Boston: Pauline Books and Media, 2006, p. 141: excerpt from the Catechesis, "Second Account of the Creation of Man", September 19, 1979, n. 4.

[59] A free translation of the adage, *sentire cum ecclesia.*

expressed in the word of God or, alternatively, it could be that there is a direct dependence of St. John Paul II on Edith Stein, St. Teresa Benedicta of the Cross; however, I cannot prove such a dependence and simply advert to it in order to indicate how the path of the Church has passed through both the work of Edith Stein and John Paul II. It is now necessary to consider some more specific features of Edith's work.

Philosophy: Edith's search for the truth led her to phenomenology: 'the world as we perceive it does not merely exist ... in our subjective perception. [Husserl's] ... pupils saw his philosophy as a return to objects: "back to things". [His] ... phenomenology unwittingly led many of his pupils to the Christian faith.[60]' In other words, there is an implicit relationship between "what is" and the Christian faith, in that truth does not contradict truth[61]; and, therefore, any philosophy which apprehends what really exists, also leads to the fullness of truth expressed in the mystery of God. At the same time, phenomenology is also an aid to philosophy itself as it helps to rescue modern thinking from an unaccountable subjectivity.

After deciding to abandon prayer, 'it was precisely along the byways of philosophical investigation that grace awaited her: having chosen to undertake the study of phenomenology, she became sensitive to an objective reality which, far from ultimately dissolving in the subject, both precedes the subject and becomes

[60] Teresa Benedicta of the Cross Edith Stein (1891-1942): http://www.vatican.va/news_services/liturgy/saints/ns_lit_doc_19981011_edith_stein_en.html.

[61] Vatican Council I, *Dei Filius*.

the measure of subjective knowledge, and thus needs to be examined with rigorous objectivity' (8)[62]. In Edith's own words: phenomenology 'turned attention away from the "subject" and toward "things" themselves'[63]. Although, it has to be said, in the very recognition of the process of perceiving the object, there is an implicit, if not an explicit, recognition of an objectified subjectivity: a recognition, in other words, of the presence of the perceiving subject as entailed in the turn 'toward "things" themselves'. Thus 'Perception again appeared as reception, deriving its laws from objects [and] not, as criticism has it, from determination which imposes its laws on the objects'[64]. Without digressing too far from Edith herself I would add, however, that perception has its own laws: it is the law of a process that provides the opportunity of an active engagement with what actually exists. In other words, perception is both a framework for making possible the active reception of what exists and, at the same time, a process through which there is a dialogue of the whole person with the reality in which we are almost seamlessly immersed.

In the temptation, as it were, of philosophical thought to emphasise one aspect of reality or another, Edith's recognition of woman's capacity for holistic human development found philosophical expression in a philosophy of wholeness. On the one

---

62 http://w2.vatican.va/content/john-paul-ii/en/motu_proprio/documents/hf_jp-ii_motu-proprio_01101999_co-patronesses-europe.html.

63 Edith Stein, *Life in a Jewish Family,* Volume One of The Collected Works, translated by Josephine Koeppel, OCD (Washington: ICS Publications, 1986), p. 250.

64 Edith Stein, *Life in a Jewish Family*, p. 250.

hand Edith says: 'The female species is characterized by the unity and wholeness of the entire psychosomatic personality and by the harmonious development of the faculties; the male species by the perfecting of individual capacities to obtain record achievements'[65]. The unfolding development of each person's characteristics, whether man or woman, clearly benefits from the reciprocal development of both human wholeness and specific capacities. On the other hand, the philosophy that attracted Edith, phenomenology, 'is an effort to "bring back into philosophy everyday things, concrete wholes, the basic experiences of life as they come to us"'[66]. In another account of phenomenology, we read that phenomenology 'describes with meticulous accuracy the stream of consciousness as it presents itself to the observing mind ... the acts performed ... for example ... in responding to a stimulus, in taking cognizance of a fact, in reaching a decision'[67]. Altogether, then, Edith Stein, and later St. John Paul II, took phenomenology's beginning with the subject's openness to phenomena of whatever kind, kindling an almost universal openness to what exists, and began to integrate it into a deeper metaphysics of what this reveals about the whole human being, relationships, reality as a whole and, ultimately, religious experience and God: 'both [Husserl and St. Thomas Aquinas]

---

[65] *Writings of Edith Stein,* selected, translated and introduced by Hilda Graef: pp. 142-143 are an extract from the "Problems of Women's Education".

[66] From Michael Novak, "John Paul II: Christian Philosopher," *America* 177: 12 (October 25, 1997), p. 12, quoted in George Weigel's, *Witness to Hope: The Biography of Pope John Paul II* (New York: Cliff Street Books, 1999), p. 127.

[67] *Writings of Edith Stein,* selected, translated and introduced by Hilda Graef: Introduction, p. 18.

considered philosophy to be an exact science that starts with the knowledge of reality through the senses and develops in intellectual activity'[68].

Clearly, however, intellectual activity runs throughout: from 'the knowledge of reality through the senses' to the development of it through 'intellectual activity'. In a certain sense, then, it is necessary to define the intellectual activity: 'Phenomenology ... taught that essences could be intuitively and immediately known without the formal apparatus of scientific method or psychological process'[69]. An essence is what is definable. Therefore, phenomenology concerns itself with an "immediate" apprehension of what exists, whether what exists is an "idea", an object or a relationship between people or all kinds of variations of these three possibilities. In other words, an actual piece of paper is 'intuitively and immediately known' as a non-living product of the labor of a person, the different kinds of which can be observed or explored with cutting, drawing or wrapping activities, the materials and processes through which it can be made can be researched; and, ultimately, the actual piece of paper can be identified as per its origin, generally or more particularly, with respect to who bought it and for how much. In other words, the object itself, "paper", implies a specifically knowable identity amidst a multitude of relationships and potential uses. This whole process implies all the psychological, sociological, philosophical, scientific and circumstantial analyses that are, in effect,

---

68 Fr. Raimondo Spiazzi, OP, "Edith Stein: St. Teresa Benedicta of the Cross", https://www.ewtn.com/library/Theology/EDITHST.HTM.

69 John C. Caiazza, "The Social Teaching of John Paul II", http://www.hprweb.com/2014/01/the-social-teaching-of-john-paul-ii/.

coextensive with the 'intuitive' definition of what exists in a particular instance and, at the same time, entails all the ramifications for the investigating subject and the whole environment of which it is a "whole" within the "whole".

Developing this interrelationship between an adequate subjectivity and a foundational understanding of the structure of being was one of the primary concerns of St. John Paul II. In other words, Edith's work was instrumental in the modern enrichment of the structure of human personhood with a more adequate account of human subjectivity, with all its unique and universal characteristics.

Judaism and feminism: In the context of anti-Semitism, which seemed to be so prevalent in what was called a country with a Christian government[70], Edith's conversion to Catholicism was also a point of re-entry into the heritage of faith which she had abandoned when she had decided to give up prayer, although she later said that 'My longing for truth was a prayer in itself'[71]. Edith did not disown her Jewish heritage and indeed it helped her to enter into the cross which was inseparable from her vocation[72].

Edith's pursuit of truth had culminated in the discovery that

[70] Cf. The words from Edith Stein's letter to Pope Pius XI in 1933 are: 'Everything that happened and continues to happen on a daily basis originates with a government that calls itself "Christian"' (p. 226 of Susanne Batzdorff's, *Aunt Edith: The Jewish Heritage of a Catholic Saint* (Springfield, Illinois: Templegate Publishers, second edition, 2003)).

[71] Mosley, *Edith Stein,* p. 64.

[72] Mosley, *Edith Stein,* pp. 46-47.

'Truth is a person, the person of Jesus [Christ]'[73]; and, at the same time, Edith followed St. Teresa of Ávila into the Catholic Church and the Carmelite order. Albeit Edith's entry into Carmel had to wait until anti-Semitism had closed all other possibilities of work to her[74] and both she and her confessor agreed that it was the providential moment for her to enter Carmel[75]. Edith's entry into Carmel, however, was not to be without the taint of a slight anti-Semitism in the course of her reception into the convent[76]. More generally, however, Edith's account of Life in a Jewish Family was to provide a real answer to the propaganda's 'horrendous caricature'[77] of Jewish people: 'to write down what I, child of a Jewish family, had learned about the Jewish people since such knowledge is so rarely found in outsiders'[78]. In the course of the dialogue between Jews and Catholics, it is almost as if the life of Edith Stein "is" a powerful catalyst of this development[79]. In the words of St. John Paul II: 'May her witness constantly strengthen the bridge of mutual understanding

---

73 Mosley, *Edith Stein*, pp. 14, but also 16.

74 Mosley, *Edith Stein*, pp. 27-28.

75 Cf. Mosley, *Edith Stein*, p.

76 Cf. Mosley, *Edith Stein*, pp. 30 and 42; however, whether this was simply anti-Semitism or the fear that Edith's Jewish background would endanger them all in an increasingly anti-Semitic climate, or both, is not clear. As regards the latter, it emerges as Edith's own concern as anti-Semitism increases: 'She was putting the community [at Cologne] at risk by her mere presence' (p. 39).

77 Edith Stein, *Life in a Jewish Family*, p. 23.

78 Stein, *Life in a Jewish Family*, p. 23.

79 Cf. Batzdorff's, *Aunt Edith*, pp. 196-211: Chapter 15: In the Spirit of Catholic-Jewish Understanding.

between Jews and Christians' (8)[80]. Furthermore, there is no doubt that her Jewish background informed her feminism and, indeed, is almost a modern forerunner to it: 'By the time [Edith's mother] was eight, she was so diligent and capable that her parents could send her to help out-of-town relatives in an emergency'[81]. In other words, although in this instance in a very "traditional" way, Edith's mother was both trained to be capable and indeed chose to be capable at a very early age[82]; and, on the death of her husband, Edith's mother was to show herself a very able businesswoman[83], providing for the education of two very able daughters[84].

Prayer and self-offering: it was the vocation of Esther, the Jewish Queen, who interceded for the salvation of her people with 'King Ahasuerus'[85], which increasingly expressed the depth of Edith's vocation: a vocation which entailed that mystery of offering her death for both persecutors and persecuted[86]. It is probably one of the deepest mysteries of the divine-human dimensions of the Christian Faith that the free act in which evil is done is the occasion through which God brings about good. Joseph, a prophetic dreamer who had been sold into slavery by his

---

80 Homily of John Paul II for the Canonization of Edith Stein.

81 Stein, *Life in a Jewish Family,* p. 37.

82 Stein, *Life in a Jewish Family,* p. 38.

83 Cf. Batzdorff's, *Aunt Edith*, p. 75.

84 Cf. Batzdorff's, *Aunt Edith*, pp. 102-110.

85 Mosley, *Edith Stein*, p. 97.

86 Mosley, *Edith Stein*, p. 97.

brothers and had yet risen to be Pharaoh's right hand man and thus was able to help his family and the whole region in a time of famine, on being reconciled with his brothers explained to them: 'you meant evil against me; but God meant it for good, to bring it about that many people should be kept alive' (Gn 50: 20). It is unavoidable, therefore, that we think of the crucifixion: that God intended for good what was clearly the dreadful death of the Son of God. In this way, therefore, Edith entered into the mystery announced, as it were, by her birth on the Jewish feast of the Atonement: the feast day of reconciliation between God and man[87].

In the dialogue between Edith Stein and Jesus Christ, we can see that Edith recognises that her vocation is a participation in the reconciling[88] self-offering of Christ. 'Edith wishes to live and die for the Church, for the concerns of Jesus and Mary, for the Order of Carmel. Then, there are the peoples to which she belongs: the communities of Cologne and Echt, the Jews and Germans, her family, friends and acquaintances. She is offering herself for all of these'[89]. Edith Stein's answer to the question of who can atone for the 'oppressed and the oppressors': it is 'the victims, willingly carrying their sufferings, who could atone'[90]. Edith was born 'in 1891, on the [Jewish feast day of the] Day of Atonement'[91] and

---

[87] Mosley, *Edith Stein*, pp. 50-51.

[88] Mosley, *Edith Stein*, p. 51.

[89] Mosley, *Edith Stein*, p. 46-47.

[90] Mosley, *Edith Stein*, p. 50.

[91] Mosley, *Edith Stein*, p. 50.

died in 'Auschwitz' in 1942[92].

At the same time Edith recognized that Christian marriage entailed an inseparable, reciprocal self-offering: 'I believe that even most of the "happy" marriages are, more often than not, at least in part a martyrdom'[93].

Conclusion

No period of history is an isolated event, either in itself or in terms of the relationship between one idea and another; and, ultimately, ideas and programmes impact on people, either bringing communion and communication or fracturing society and imperilling the lives of people. Our times are very much an outcome of the mentality which is, in a certain sense, radically incapable of recognising the equality of all human beings in the gift of human personhood. Just as the "structure of energy" is manifest in the capabilities of matter and its states, whether solid, liquid or gas, so the visible more generally communicates the invisible; and, as such, the psychological is inherent in the embryological development of the human person: the relationship of mother and father to their child is already as "psychologically existent" as it is physiologically drawn upon in conception.

What we witness, however, in the life of Edith Stein, is that the last word of human development goes to the Christian mystery of the "gift of self": the reciprocal gift of self between Edith Stein and

---

92 Mosley, *Edith Stein*, p. 56.

93 Mosley, *Edith Stein*, p. 82, quoting from: *Die Frau: Fragestellungen und Reflexionen* (Freiburg, Basle and Vienna: Herder, 2000), p. 50.

Jesus Christ. Even if in the course of her life she espoused all the good developments of a true, realistic type of feminism, unfolding profound philosophical and personal gifts, the "leaven" of Edith's life goes on unfolding in the most influential way through the very Jewish-Christian identity that expresses the deepest contours of the path of life.

I am personally grateful, then, for the opportunity to begin to draw on her participation in the dialogue of our times; and, in so far as I have been able, I hope this article encourages others to turn to this modern Mother of the Church.

There now follow three experiences from the pilgrimage to Cracow. Grace is an undergraduate at Cambridge University, studying Human Social and Political Science. Peter is at secondary school and enjoys literary subjects, artistic ventures and sporty stuff. Teresa is the second year of 'A' levels and is planning to study psychology at university.

Grace, Teresa and Peter Etheredge

World Youth Day Pilgrimage Experiences (Cracow, 2016)

Grace Etheredge
Identity and the Experience of the World - Youth Day Pilgrimage to Cracow

I am a Catholic.

This is a statement that is not often heard to pass the lips of a

19 year old. For two weeks however, in Holland, Germany and then Poland, to hear this was nothing unusual.

On the weekend of Saturday the 1st of August, 2.5 million young people gathered in Kraków, Poland, to listen to the Holy Father and to celebrate mass with him. This was the climax of a 12-day pilgrimage which had spanned four countries.

Our journey began in Mile End, London, where 450 people from all over Britain met to receive the sacrament of reconciliation. With eager anticipation of the events ahead, we then set off for Dover, to take the ferry to France. Unfortunately, God had decided to offer a unique ice-breaker experience for all of the pilgrims - a two day traffic jam which gave us the perfect opportunity to get to know each other. Feeling a little like the Israelites after nearly 40 hours in the desert, we eventually made it to Dover, landing in France for an overnight stay on the coach. It was in this truck park, where we spent the night, where we were to have one of the most beautiful masses of the pilgrimage. Encircled by trucks, and a picnic table for an altar, we were able to bless God for our safe arrival and receive communion at the end of a very challenging ordeal.

The pilgrimage gave us the opportunity to do many things and visit many places, not least the Holocaust Memorial of Berlin and the Salt Mines of Wieliczka, but one visit stood out for me in particular as being very powerful. This was the visit to the Auschwitz Museum, the location of the infamous concentration camps. Split into two separate camps, the Auschwitz site was appalling in its size but, with regards to Auschwitz I, also appalling in its apparent normality. Built in a very modern style, the red brick buildings were lined with avenues of trees. It could have been a school. The only signs of the horror the complex had seen, were the information boards that documented the atrocities committed and the barbed wire that topped the fencing. Initially, the beauty of the trees contrasted with the pain embedded in the architecture made me feel extremely uncomfortable. However, I was able to take solace from the presence of such greenery as I realised, from the pictures of Auschwitz in use, how the trees and plants had been cut down or destroyed. The growth of them now, in the present, after the closure of the camps, demonstrated to me how good could conquer evil. Maximilian Kolbe's witness to God, as he sacrificed his life for that of a father, also reinforced how God brings good out of evil and gave me hope for the present day conflicts in Syria and beyond, where a new generation of people are being persecuted. The fact that pain exists at all in this world is something that I, personally, have struggled to reconcile with any kind of faith at all as how can God permit the people he loves to suffer? My visit to Auschwitz helped me to confront this question, and did not completely banish my doubts, but reconciled me to the belief that people are not put into extraordinary situations to destroy them, but to give them the opportunity, as Maximilian Kolbe had been given, to encounter God.

The experience of the World Youth Day weekend was made all the more powerful by our experiences of Auschwitz as, for two days, people from all over the world were brought together, not to suffer, but to rejoice and to join in community and solidarity with one another. Traversing the fifteen kilometres of the bus stop to the camp site, I met people of all nationalities, French Catholics, Malaysian Charismatics and even American nuns, whose enthusiastic singing of Justin Bieber's greatest hits kept us marching at a good and steady pace.

The candlelit vigil of the Saturday night was another of my favourite moments as the Pope encouraged all people to get out and do something with their lives. Having seen the potential that mankind has for unbelievable acts of evil, the Pope's call for unbelievable acts of goodness was a very powerful message to hear.

Three weeks later, it is still not often that I even hear myself speak the words, "I am a Catholic", but the moments when I do are testament to my experience in Poland: an experience that was truly incredible.

A combined account by Peter (Part I) and Teresa Etheredge (Part II)

Peter Etheredge: Part I: Days 1-6 of 12 The World Youth Day Pilgrimage

We had been fundraising for this event for a long time, roughly eleven to twelve months, selling in a number of parishes cakes that we hope were enjoyed. This is an account by two of the pilgrims who travelled to Poland and Kraków to meet the Pope and participate in World Youth Day 2016, entailing a stunning pilgrimage to go with it.

Days 1 to 6 of 12

On Friday, 22nd of July, pilgrims from all over England converged on London where we gathered in some church for a penitential. Going out the way we came, we grabbed our luggage and lugged it over this massive road and gave it to these guys who loaded it onto the seven coaches. We shared our coach with an outskirts-of-London-community, Bedford.

Having had a packed dinner, we set off from London through the night in the general direction of Dover. To our annoyance, we were stuck in a gigantic snaking traffic jam which halted our progress considerably. Walking alongside the coach, which would move about five metres every twenty minutes, we envied very un-Christianly the three coaches which had slipped through and caught the ferry that morning to get well on their way to Amsterdam. As a result of the traffic, we actually missed our ferry and got on the following one after a long slog down some obscure motorway. Unfortunately, this meant that we wouldn't be able to get to Amsterdam in time to do anything substantial, much to our disappointment.

After entering mainland Europe from the ferry, featuring a good, unhealthy, English, mound of fish and chips I might add, we waited in Calais for a while, where we played hand cricket, sat around, said prayers, or threw hats at each other and generally got to know the Bedford community better. Crossing from France into Belgium, we stopped in a lorry park for the drivers to get a good nine hour sleep from their labour so they could drive again onto Germany; everyone else sleeping too. In the morning, we had mass in a nearby field, receiving the word, communion and weird looks from the natives. After lunch, we moved on again for Germany, arriving late at night in Berlin, after a dinner in McDonalds or its supermarket neighbour, where we hauled our luggage from the coach and into a hotel for the night, slipping gratefully into showers and falling asleep before we hit the bed. Some of us more resilient people went straight to the pool for a late night swim.

On the Monday morning, we had a fabulous and much needed breakfast which wasn't a sandwich as we had been living off recently and were immediately dragged into the coaches once again; driving through the well lined streets to the centre of Berlin and fell into the shadow of its towering skyscrapers. Walking into a huge park, we sat down in the shade of a few trees and the head catechist of the English pilgrims gave us a catechesis on Europe, dwelling on Nazism and Communism. He then moved on to the present atrocities that have developed concerning how certain scientists have turned conception into a lab procedure, treating humanity as a test product devoid of respect or value as a human person – through branches such as IVF. He spoke of the future of the world and how modern society affects the upbringing of children, such as through the separation that excessive use of social media creates in the home between the user and their family and friends. It was quite a frightening speech. Processing out of the park by the way us pilgrim walkers do, we arrived at the Memorial to the Murdered Jews of Europe – an acre of concrete blocks, shaped like tombstones that grew in height from about half a foot or flat at the edges to fifteen feet in the centre. All grew solemn as we wandered through the place, ending our song and banter, in the shadow of Nazism beneath the burning sun. After about an hour, we moved on to the square where we dispersed for lunch and then went out to find out the historical view of Berlin's colourful past.

When we arrived back at the hotel some hours later, we had an hour free to lounge about before dinner and many descended straight into the swimming pool, which was only about four feet deep, and chaos ensued. After a lovely dinner and many compliments to the chefs, we changed into our best clothes and went outside for mass. The mass was just as the sun set so everything was as beautiful as masses should be, with pilgrims standing up to give their experience of their journey of faith after the gospel, and ending with a dance and a hymn well into the night.

Tuesday morning, we set out from the Berlin hotel and crossed into Poland and Wroclaw, the city of Polish saint and martyr Edith Stein. Evangelising in the city centre, we danced and listened to a few more experiences of the Way and then retired to various hostels across the city, had dinner and collapsed into bed.

Wednesday, we left the university hostel we were assigned to after a filling breakfast and arrived in Auschwitz 1. We disembarked from the coaches and, after much queuing, we entered through a tall arch of twisted metal, bearing the phrase, "Work sets us free" in German – a cold mockery of the hundreds of thousands of victims of the camp. The first thing that greeted us was the unsettling normality of the place; the houses were redbrick with windows. It seemed wrong that the place that had slaughtered more innocents than we can comprehend looked so... peaceful. Silently, we roamed the buildings, reading placards that described the horrors each building had been used for and almost not believing that this village-size place could be a machine of such carnage. Auschwitz 2, Birkenau, was only a little different, with less houses and more rolling fields. Another thing was the silence; it was everywhere and seemed never to be broken despite the talk and the murmurs. In each field were pits or strange chimneys with a trough leading up to it, the foundations for buildings in long rows. The great fences of merciless wire, nails and posts were always in sight, the only indications of the prison this place was. We said a prayer for all the people who had been murdered within these grounds.

After Auschwitz, we ate a quick lunch and were on the coaches again, heading for Fr Mariusz's Parish. Gathered in a great hall, we were given a talk on the church we were in and how, through the efforts of Pope John Paul the 2nd under Communism before he became Pope. Afterwards, we were shown the film "Karol", a production on the life of the Pope and the tragic drama that it entails. For dinner, tables of food had been set up while we were watching, much to our delight. Then, we got on our coaches and drove back to our hostels and collapsed once more into our beds, emotionally and physically exhausted.

Teresa Etheredge: Part II: Days 7-12 of 12
The World Youth Day Pilgrimage

Day 7 to 12 of 12

On Thursday 28th, the coaches turned towards a beautiful white-washed complex set out on the side of a mountain. This was the Czerna Carmelite Monastery. Beneath a huge stained glass crucifix and surrounded by images of saints, we learnt about the theologian and philosopher Edith Stein who had been such an inspiration to Pope John Paul II. Hearing about her birth in Wroclaw, Poland as a German Jew, her conversion to Christianity and her eventual death in the Nazi concentration camps, it was no surprise she was canonized as a martyr to become St Teresa Benedicta of the Cross.

Later that same day, 350 pilgrims descended upon the salt mines of Wieliczka where a guided tour revealed the shimmering majesty of sculptures, chasms, lakes and an enormous awe-inspiring cathedral hewn directly from the rock salt. Three miners, one after the other, had taken a total of 67 years to carve reliefs, statues and even chandeliers from the salt whenever they were off duty. The magnificent result threw yesterday's time in Auschwitz into painful contrast: that people just like us could do things so incredibly horrific and so incredibly amazing is a startling realization.

Friday was a gorgeous day of sunshine and soft breezes. Karol Wojtyla, when still only a simple priest, had been fond of the mountain outside Wisla and often enjoyed the calm pleasure of country walks there. We sort-of followed his example, going up the mountain to relax and enjoy ice-creams and the view, except we cheated and rode a chair lift rather than walking. Our time was very peaceful and chilled, ending with a lovely (although grasshopper-infested) Mass on the side of the mountain.

And then on the Sabbath day, Saturday 30th July, the long-awaited vigil with the Holy Father was looming, anticipation blemished only by the knowledge of the 8-mile walk necessary to reach our campsite. Despite being ravaged by hay fever, as we staggered under our backpacks and sweated in the relentless sun, the walk was actually quite fun. Flags waved over the hordes of cheerful Christians; hymns and Justin Bieber alike were sung in languages of all the nations as we were drenched by the hosepipes and sprinkler systems of sympathetic Poles.

Upon arriving at Sector A14, we set ourselves up and then amused ourselves, being provided with blue bags of food, bottled water and an insane amount of radishes. I still don't understand the radishes although I quite enjoyed them, being like a bright pink cross between apples and onions. People from everywhere were around us, groups of joking Irish and praying Texans (we interrupted and then joined them for evening prayer) and Brazilians who gave us even more radishes. As the sun began to descend and the air grew cooler, the religious pop music we had been blasted with all afternoon finally began to silence.

The Pope's service began with the experiences of several young people who had been helped through the Catholic church, including a drug addict and a shell-shocked Syrian. We prayed together, and then Pope Francis began to speak. He talked of the plight of young people today, how we confuse comfort with happiness, how we allow ourselves to live a life of stagnation and insignificance. He urged us to stop being couch potatoes, to come out of our self-inflicted isolation and make a mark on the world. He described the lives many of us live, locked away in our bedrooms, playing games and messaging friends while we ignore everyone else around us. The Holy Father's speech was followed by a peaceful time of candle-lit reflection, which then ended rather abruptly with another round of Catholic rock music. This did not quieten until well into the night, so my little group sat around talking, eating radishes and playing Truth or Dare with various people who wandered along.

The next morning, we were wakened bright and early at around 6:00am by engineers testing the sound systems. The air was already humid and warm, and it quickly grew into a heat even greater than the day before. After feasting on a breakfast of ice cream, hot dogs and porridge, we sat around alternately envying those who still slept and pouring water on our heads to keep cool. The Mass began later that day. It was a beautiful service, particularly characterized by a beautiful homily. The gospel had been the story of Zacchaeus and Pope Francis talked about the three things which held us back from God: first, Zacchaeus' small stature, which symbolises our fear of our own unworthiness. Second, climbing the tree; we must not be afraid of ridicule or of making our faith obvious, as the risk we take to find Jesus is truly worth it. The third obstacle between us and God are those around us: in Zacchaeus' case, the angry townsfolk who believed he could never better himself. These problems, great as they can seem, nonetheless can be overcome if only we believe God loves us. With God anything is possible.

The last day of our pilgrimage saw a visit to the John Paul II centre, yet another sweaty day that ended with a serene Mass in an interestingly octagonal chapel. And then we went back to the hostel.

And then we went home.

We would like to thank everyone who bought cakes and candles and jam at our various sales, and a special thank you to everyone who gave us donations. The trip was definitely worth it, and we are very grateful.

Saint Teresa Benedicta of the Cross (Edith Stein)

Courtesy of Wikipedia

Chapter Four

Traversing Life

General Introduction to Chapter 4: Pilgrim. There comes a point, then, when being an unconscious pilgrim changed, whether or not through actual pilgrimages, and I began to see that I needed the help of God; indeed that death, whatever kind of doorway it will be, helps us to recognize that we are a part of a great exodus: a passing of people from slavery to freedom: from being estranged from others to being fit for friendship: from an unwillingness to live forgiveness to love's possibility of the gift of eternal life. Thus there is, as it were, a passage to being a pilgrim. On the one hand this book charts, in a way, the very passage to pilgrimage: from an almost inbuilt restlessness to consciously hoping in the Word of God; but, on the other hand, this particular chapter takes us through the traversal of a life that shows, as clearly as life-changes can, that becoming a pilgrim enables us to see that God "completes" the work of "becoming ourselves". It is not as if the hardships will necessarily cease, or indeed the need to pray come to an end, but it is at least clear that life is going towards eternity.

Or to put it the other way round: we are being drawn through time to eternity.

One of "life's-questions", as it were, is whether or not to marry, to be a monk or a priest; and, as it transpires, a central theme of this pilgrimage from a multitude of uncertainties was, in fact, being able to marry and to unfold a family life. At the same time, as we shall see in the final chapter, another of "life's-questions" is what work belongs to me to do: a question that ran throughout the years of the Life-Cycle prose poems and continues to call me to pray and to work. A third question, inseparable to the other two and more prominently expressed in this chapter is the relationship between vocation and conversion: conversion brought clarity about vocation.

This chapter begins, then, with a personal history of coming to marriage: of coming to marriage through all kinds of suffering (I). Secondly, there is a more developed exploration of how experience informs our understanding of the accompaniment that is so frequently necessary to people returning to the sacrament of matrimony or indeed being embraced by it (II). Finally, there is how to make sense of one of the ongoing questions in our time: Is there a real human nature and how does it express itself in "influencing" our concrete choices (III)?

Part I: On Coming to the Sacrament of Marriage

Introduction to Chapter 4: Part I: On Coming to the Sacrament of Marriage[94]. In the context of the widespread discussion on how to help married people, whether in the preparation for marriage, in the midst of difficulties or in the impossible moments of coming to the truth about marriage, I saw the need to draw on my own experience of how God has helped me to both recognise my own vocation and to inform this debate with the reality of experience: a reality that witnesses to the mercy of God as greater than the wretchedness of the sinner.

"On the Truth that Heals (cf. Jn 8: 31-32) the Crisis of Marriage"

The truth to be uncovered, however, is nothing if it is not what we recognise in our hearts. When Jesus Christ said to the woman at the well, 'he whom you now have is not your husband' (Jn 4: 18), it was not a truth that she rejected or rebelled against; rather, in her experience of life, it was a word which delivered her from the many faceted difficulties of identifying what was going on (cf. Jn 4: 7-26). At the same time, Christ turned her to a new understanding of communicating with the Father 'in spirit and truth' (Jn 4: 24); and, in the very reality of the word which He

---

94 Fr. David Meconi has now taken this piece for publication in April, 2018, on the Homiletic and Pastoral Review website: http://www.hprweb.com/author/francis-etheredge/.

spoke to her, Christ established her in the truth which made it possible for her to worship the Father 'in spirit and truth' (Jn 4: 24). While, on the one hand, we do not know what happened to the Samaritan woman, we do know that the Lord brought about salvation in her life. On the other hand, even if we do not know how her life ended, we can trust that because she accepted that Christ had led her to 'the Father', bringing others with her (Jn 4: 21, 23, 27-42), that the Father welcomed her into His kingdom, along with those her witness had brought to Him.

This article, therefore, is about my experience of coming to the truth of marriage: an experience that was long and painful and, at the same time, an unaccountably intimate dialogue with the truth about myself; and, in that respect, the call to prayer is about precisely the person that I am coming into the presence of God and asking for help in the "today" of my life (cf. Ps 95: 7). God, however, speaks the truth in a way that, ultimately, leads to a heart that can hope in His help; and, like the woman at the well, the history that brought me to Him is a prelude to being clear that He has made a new beginning in the life that, ultimately, He began and never abandoned.

There are the following three parts to this account of the help that Christ and His Church can give to us. Part A: On a Personal History of Coming to Marriage; Part B: On the Trials of Marriage; and, Part C: On two Temptations in Responding to Real Difficulties.

Part A: On a Personal History of Coming to Marriage

While it was obvious to many, if not to all, that marriage was one of a variety of human possibilities, my experience of coming to the possibility of marriage, several times, and being unable to marry, reveals that both in terms of this generation and the particular characteristics of my own history, marriage turned out to be far from a self-evident option. The point, then, of this introductory section is to show, however briefly, that the word and action of God has been a necessary ingredient in becoming clear, chaste and capable of being open to the full reality of marriage.

In the beginning, then, as a girl-friend emerged out of an indiscriminate mass of people, so began a heartbreaking search for the nature of what it was all about.

On the one hand there were a number of women, over the years, without any clarity as to what determined the possibility of marrying one rather than another, except that often there were complicating factors; and, indeed, those complicating factors could be anything from an existing, previous or potential marriage to someone else, to the perplexing and bewildering basic questions about marriage as a "closed" cell: an unalterable one to one sentence. Not to mention the difficulties, if not human impossibility, of possessing a stable identity, a means of earning a living or even an understanding of what defined marriage as an expression of human friendship. Even if it was clear that an annulment, a formal recognition by the Catholic Church that a particular couple were not sacramentally married, it was nevertheless unclear what constituted the choice of a spouse: what differentiated one person from another.

On the other hand, it was abundantly obvious that the pain of human experience taught that the desire to marry was almost irrepressible and sprang afresh even after many anxious, fraught and bitter disappointments; and, at the same time, the Catholic culture of being open to life was challenged, even among Catholic religious, to the point of making the search for the truth an imperative for a broken but indeterminate Catholic-Christian: a Christian who did not understand his own complete inability to identify and to live a Christian life. In the very process of drawing close to the Catholic Church it became clear that, confused and uncertain about marriage, marrying a divorcee in a registry office did not address the freedom to marry or the reality of marriage as the whole gift of self; however, a part of coming to that conclusion was being refused absolution in confession because it was not at all clear, to me or to the priest, that I had rejected the possibility of marrying in a registry office.

From the depths of human experience

There emerged, then, a certain logic from the depths of human experience; and, even if this was not equivalent to salvation, yet it did, remotely, begin to point to the path of truth towards it. Firstly, it was increasingly obvious that whatever "faith" was, it was not obvious to me; and, therefore, without fully grasping this ignorance, my life as a Catholic-Christian was almost a "seesaw" between sin and the sacrament of reconciliation.

Secondly, the natural history of a disordered life raised the question of a psychological condition that arose from denying the humiliations which were suffered at school; however, as the probing continued, so it "made sense" that the internal disorder that needed discovering was expressed in an outward disorder which constantly showed itself in abandoned courses, short term work and an inconclusive work and vocational identity. In terms of answering the question of the origin of psychological disorders, nothing was as adequate as the origin of original sin: a sin that simultaneously deprived human beings of the complete gift of the Creator and, at the same time, originated the development of the imperfections which manifest themselves in dysfunctional human lives.

Thirdly, impoverished friendships, uncertainties about identity, the readiness to give and to take in the giving, left a person swirling amidst a multitude of ideas which were partial truths and "moments" that disintegrated into nothing. As impossible as it was to fulfil, the desire for permanence shone through all the transitory relationships. Indeed, love began to make sense as a single act of loving another person: as if the equality of love, of a man loving and being loved by a woman, transcended all the other imperfections of actual concrete people. The constant problem, however, was the restless inability to "commit" to one person.

Fourthly, the whole disaster of contraception and abortion rose up, like a rebellion, protesting the existence of human life and the profoundly open and uncompromised gift of self which belonged to marriage; but, again, the impossibility of transcending almost endemic "transitoriness" did nothing but rage like a nature at war with itself and threatened, increasingly, the reality of life and hope itself.

Finally: How many visits to confessors, spiritual directors or advisers, even a so called Christian psychotherapist, did nothing to root order in a disordered heart; and, therefore, there grew a profound dichotomy between an increasingly explicit understanding of the Christian vision of the human person and, paradoxically, a personal ignorance of sin and the call to conversion.

A powerfully gentle word that brought the change it expressed

A word of God transforms a life in a way completely different to the truth that emerges, nonetheless, from a disordered life. Indeed, the truth that does emerge from experience is still true, but it is like a laser that does not cut: it does not bring with it that power to change that is as inseparable to the word of God as the beginning of creation. Thus there was a moment in which death had found its prey; indeed, having failed to take my life at fourteen, it was revisiting the possibility at forty, having failed many times in between. It is difficult to account for the difference between a "being-for-death" and a "being-for-life"; but, in a moment, Christ passed through the closed door of my heart and fulfilled the words I read in the *Catechism of the Catholic Church*: 'Since God could create everything out of nothing, he can also, through the Holy Spirit, give spiritual life to sinners by creating a pure heart in them ... '(CCC, 298). Within twelve months I married. Twenty years later, we have ten children, two of whom are in heaven, and the power of that word still unfolds through many other words within the Word.

Faith and the Sacrament of Marriage[95]

When I consider the "times" I have tried to marry, and failed, and the growing awareness, even if I resisted the truth of it, that the reason was that I had no faith, I begin to see that "no faith" is evidenced in that fact that I was unable to marry: of being unable to enter a "place" I imagined to be a place of inescapable suffering. I could not "force" myself, in other words, to go through an impassable barbed wire entrance; and, therefore, I remained unmarried. The evidence of faith, then, was expressed in the fact of being able to marry, however frail and anxious about the prospect I actually felt.

Whether, more widely, a marriage, 'though celebrated in Church, is to be considered invalid due to the absence of faith'[96] needs further consideration; indeed, the very presence of the man and the woman in a Church, receiving the sacrament of marriage, could imply the "minimum" of faith that St. John Paul II recognised for the validity of marriage: 'that faith towards which the married couple are already journeying by reason of the uprightness of their intention, which Christ's grace certainly does not fail to favor and support' (Familiaris Consortio, 68). On the one hand, then, there is the positive sense of marrying with a right intention, 'even if not in a fully conscious way'; thus, St. John Paul

---

95 A new, albeit brief section, is here added to the published article.

96 Andrea Tornielli, "Müller, Buttiglione and the "confusion" of those criticizing the Pope",
http://www.lastampa.it/2017/11/07/vaticaninsider/eng/documents/mller-buttiglione-and-the-confusion-of-those-criticizing-the-pope-PpxFQoXlPfNiV4WFzk8koJ/pagina.html.

II says: 'the decision of a man and a woman to marry in accordance with this divine plan, that is to say, the decision to commit by their irrevocable conjugal consent their whole lives in indissoluble love and unconditional fidelity, really involves, even if not in a fully conscious way, an attitude of profound obedience to the will of God, an attitude which cannot exist without God's grace' (*Familiaris Consortio*, 68). But, on the other hand, not wishing to 'lay down ... criteria that would concern the level of faith of those to be married' (*Familiaris Consortio*, 68), does raise the question of what explicitly challenges the validity of marriage. Thus St. John Paul II goes on to say: 'when in spite of all efforts, engaged couples show that they reject explicitly and formally what the Church intends to do when the marriage of baptized persons is celebrated, the pastor of souls cannot admit them to the celebration of marriage' (*Familiaris Consortio*, 68).

In general, then, discerning the reality of a person's intention to marry is indeed a necessary but not a rigorously exhausting task. In other words, in my experience, even being able to marry is an expression of faith: faith in God who can act even in the light of a history that would definitely counsel against the wisdom of marrying.

Part B: On the Trials of Marriage

It is almost impossible to count the number of trials in a marriage. Indeed, almost anything, beginning and ending with money, ill health, work-related stresses, studying, seeking work, a home for a growing family, being open to life, relatives and old friends, seeking comfort or understanding in a difficult time, never mind the additional challenges of extra money for car repairs, Christmas presents and the general wear and exhausting nature of a young family, can all be the occasion of marital difficulties. The prospect of divorce, adultery, separation, returning to the parental home, abandoning the family, "going lost", drinking or any of an almost unimaginable variety of ways of falling prey to the daily impossibilities of marriage and family life, all of which help to discover in "each of us" the human weakness and tendency to reject and recoil from the sufferings of an intense daily life. Whether the difficulty was brief, serious, long-term, personal, shared or a complex combination of a whole variety of factors, the ongoing, daily reality of life did not entail sweeping changes but almost imperceptibly gradual modifications of heart, circumstances and life-style. The visit of an angel to Joseph, then, which helped him to accept the reality of Mary's miraculous pregnancy (cf. Mt 1: 18-25), is also a sign of the divine help that we all need in the course of married life – even from its beginnings and until its very end.

What, then, is the principle help to married people, including preparing for marriage, marrying, founding a family and unfolding the myriad daily difficulties that are a part of the multifaceted reality of life? Accompaniment, as it is called, has specific roots in the chaplaincy work of Karol Wojtyla: 'Wojtyla ... thought of his chaplaincy as a ministry of "accompaniment", a way to "accompany" these students in their lives': 'A really effective chaplaincy, he believed, had to be present to these young lives in the world as well as in the Church'[97]. Thus the "accompanying" went on into the lives of those who married, were open to life and who continued in this developing spirituality which unfolded in the ministry of Wojtyla (later John Paul II)[98]. This pastoral experience, then, as curate as well as Pope, gradually convinced John Paul II of the necessity of World Youth Days: 'that a pastoral strategy of "accompaniment" with young people was as valid for a pope as it had been for a fledgling priest'[99]. Accompaniment is also a characteristic of a small community sharing prayer, the word of God and the help of periodic times of retreat or convivance[100]; and, more recently, "accompaniment" has been identified in different ways in Pope Francis', the Joy of Love[101]: on the many and diverse ways of helping people celebrate marriage and family life.

In a word, then, the action of God did two, if not three things. The patience of God allowed me to reach the point of being ready to receive the help of God. However, in retrospect, the help of God had been available in many ways, throughout my entire life; and,

97 George Weigel, *Witness to Hope: The Biography of Pope John Paul II,* (New York: Cliff Street Books (an imprint of HarperCollins*Publishers*), 1999), p. 100.

98 Cf. Weigel, *Witness to Hope*, pp. 100-108.

99 Weigel, *Witness to Hope*, p. 493.

100 Eg. As found in the Neocatechumenal Way.

101 Cf. Pope Francis, Chapter 6 of *Amoris Laetitia,* http://w2.vatican.va/content/dam/francesco/pdf/apost_exhortations/documents/papa-francesco_esortazione-ap_20160319_amoris-laetitia_en.pdf; indeed, the reality of accompaniment is such a rich and complex phenomenon, as much about the family being accompanied sharing that experience, as other families and people accompanying them.

therefore, what was different was that there was a moment when this was experienced as an inner certainty: that God helps. In the course of marriage, then, the turn to prayer and the grace to believe that God acted in the circumstances of our life, made it possible for us to be open to life, even in the midst of our various sufferings. Thus there was the steady turn to prayer and the benefit of various kinds of help. Secondly, the presence of a walking community, a group of people to whom the word of God was also being addressed, was a constant source of help as well as, in its own way, a source of many challenges too. Finally, God had gone before us and raised up a charism of the Catholic Church which accompanied us in many different ways, and still does: the Neocatechumenal Way.

The reality of conversion is not magic, however, and moves in a mysterious way amidst the warp and weave of actual lives, circumstances and possibilities. While it is possible to emphasize or over-emphasise one help or remedy over another, there is no doubt that the constant help of word, liturgy and community throw light on the "every day" nature of the Christian Faith and its being lived; and, at the same time, exposes the truth that Christ is present in marriage in a way that can only be described as constantly turning water into wine (cf. Jn 2: 5-11). In other words, then, it is possible to discover that the "life of Christ" is not just a kind of religious ornament on the human nature of marriage – but that the presence of Christ is what constantly makes possible the passage from death to life in the communion of marriage and family life.

Part C: Two Temptations to Polarisation

It is possible, then, to widen particular difficulties and to pose a tension, as it were, between doctrine and pastoral experience: as if doctrinal truth and pastoral experience can be opposed to one another in the one Church of Christ – as if love and truth are not inseparable in Christ and His Church. The value of this exercise is to explore the danger of division in an otherwise necessary dialogue about the subtleties of the truth entailed in real experience.

The objectivity of the truth

On the one hand, then, it could be claimed that there is a tendency to recognise that the truth is, by definition, incontrovertible. Therefore, if an action is a sin of adultery then that, of itself, determines the objective nature of the act; and, although 'intention' and 'circumstance' can intensify or alleviate the degree of personal responsibility, neither intention nor circumstance can change a sin into a good act[102]. As it says in the Catechism: 'There are acts which, in and of themselves, independently of circumstances and intentions, are always gravely illicit by reason of their object; such as blasphemy and perjury, murder and adultery' (CCC, 1756). In other words, presuming the conditions necessary to the reality of a marriage, supernaturally constituted through the baptismal faith of the man and woman, there is an act as irrevocable as the Incarnation, Death and

[102] Cf. *Catechism of the Catholic Church,* (CCC), 1749-1756.

Resurrection of Jesus Christ: an act which gives life through death in marriage.

We might say, therefore, that there is the possibility of emphasizing the reality of living in the truth in a way that it is impossible to envisage how the sinner can come to it. It is not, therefore, that the truth of the sacrament of marriage is open to change, or that there can be an understanding of sin that contradicts sound reason, Revelation and Magisterial discernment and Tradition; rather, it is a question of whether or not it is possible to communicate the splendour of the truth in a way which contradicts the spirit of love: that the truth be expressed as a heartless measure of the impossibility of human effort, the quagmire of human difficulties and the tragic ramifications of consequences which continue to unfold.

Doctrinal and dogmatic truths are not, however, unassailable towers impossible for human beings to scale; rather, they are an expression of the interior life of God which He alone makes possible in the life of a sinner and of the Church. Thus there is, as it were, an echo of the life of the Blessed Trinity in the very mysteries of the Church which God alone makes possible for us to bear within us as the evidence of His own existence and active presence among us.

Thus the temptation of this tendency is to overlook the fact that the lived reality of being a Christian is a gift of God; and, in truth, it is the love of God which makes the sinner a resplendent member of His Church. Therefore, in front of the impossibility of living love's truth, it is absolutely necessary to discover the poverty (cf. Ps 34: 6) that makes it possible for the power of God to deliver from sin and to open a way through the impossibilities of life (cf.

Ex 14: 15 - 15: 22). Is there, at the heart of this temptation, an uncertainty about the "power" of God to act and to bring life out of death; and, therefore, is there a real need to rediscover the grace of God in action?

The grace of God acts in the reality of "today"

On the other hand, then, it could be argued that there is a pastoral, Christ-like touch that enables a person to come out of his present situation and to start walking with Him. It is not, therefore, about telling Mary Magdalene or the nameless men in her life that there are human impossibilities, such as the quandaries of what to do in the context of divorce, remarriage, adultery, the renunciation of sex in an unlawful union or multiple partners. Rather, it is about communicating that Christ said that 'apart from me you can do nothing' (Jn 15: 5): that there is a reality to the deliverance from sin that only God can give to a person who is either unable to see, objectively, the truth of his situation or, further, having glimpsed the truth of it is unable to come out of it. In other words, no amount of parish programmes, theses or dogmatic truths, on their own, can bring about God's action in the human heart; however, there is no certainty that God will not act through parish programmes, theses or dogmatic truths and, therefore, they cannot be automatically discontinued or abandoned. What is more, Christ said to a public sinner, indeed, to anyone who is disposed to listen to His word: "go, and do not sin again" (Jn 8: 11). In other words, the word of Christ is a word of power.

In the context of the present climate, perhaps we need to

recognise the extra-sacramental action of God which belongs, in fact, to the liturgy of the Church[103]: the liturgy that proclaims and makes possible the Passover from death to life: through conversion to the good forgotten, obscured or forsaken in sin. In view, then, of the whole of life, there is the possibility that God can use anything and everything to draw the sinner to Himself and to help him, little by little, to live in Him. Does not St. Augustine say that the greatness of God is shown precisely through what scandalizes us: that God allows sin because He can bring good out of it? God, however, does not sin; but God does take the sin of the sinner and help him to discover the lie that needs love in the truth to be healed.

Thus the temptation of this tendency is to overlook that the messiness of life is a point of departure; and, what is more, that a point of departure entails an ongoing action of God which is as beautifully true as it is God acting to bring His love to exist. Indeed, it is possible to reproach the sinner so forcefully for his sin as to abandon hope in the heart so bruised that the tendency to repentance is rejected as too painful and the Church as too unwelcoming; and, therefore, it is possible that this betrays an unwillingness to see the mercy of God as actively bringing about the very dialogue which, paradoxically, can rebound against the sinner[104]. In other words, there needs to be a renewal in Christ who, in the mystery of the Church, comes in search of the sinner; but, in the very nature of His coming, brings a change in the very

---

[103] Cf. Pope Benedict's XVI, *Verbum Domini*, nn. 84-87.

[104] Cf. Pope Francis, "Pope's Morning Homily: Chief Priests Rejected a Repentant Judas", December 13th, 2016, https://zenit.org/articles/popes-morning-homily-chief-priests-rejected-a-repentant-judas/ .

person to whom He comes.

The truth in love and the action of the word and grace of God

In a word, then, perhaps there is not so much a divisive difference as the need to listen to the "other" in the articulation of our faith[105]; and, together, to show that Christ calls us all, wherever we are, whether in a mess or not, to shine through with the gratuitous nature of His love-gift of salvation. As St. John Paul II said in his homily for the canonization of Edith Stein: 'St Teresa Benedicta of the Cross says to us all: Do not accept anything as the truth if it lacks love. And do not accept anything as love which lacks truth! One without the other becomes a destructive lie'[106]. On the one hand Christ's love of the Church is the basis of the 'indissolubility of the marriage bond'; and, on the other hand, Christ comes to help couples as the 'physician' of the sick (Mt 9: 12). This is the heart of the question: to find a way, in accordance with the 'indissolubility of the marital bond', to bring the help of Christ to couples. What, then, is true love's answer? In part, true love's answer depends on the word and grace of God; and, in part, true love's answer depends on the pastoral reality of the 'couples' who are seeking the help of Christ and His Church[107].

---

[105] Cf. Cardinal Peter Turkson, Edward Pentin's, "Church Leaders Respond to the 'Dubia'", December 6th, 2016, http://www.ncregister.com/daily-news/church-leaders-respond-to-the-dubia

[106] Sunday, 11th October, 1998, n. 6.

[107] Francis Etheredge's Response on LinkedIn, 9/12/16, to Edward Pentin's, "Church Leaders Respond to the 'Dubia'", December 6th, 2016.

What, then, are the parameters of the action of God, not because God is restricted but because He has already declared Himself through the voice of the Church? In the response of the Church to the actual situations in which people find themselves, it has already been authoritatively said: 'It must be discerned with certainty by means of the external forum established by the Church whether there is objectively such a nullity of marriage'[108]. In other words, there is a need for the objective expression of an annulment in the external forum of the Church if, that is, a marriage is to be declared as sacramentally invalid; and, if sacramentally invalid, not binding on those who had entered into it.

The word of the Lord

Conversely, then, the action of God which is unbounded is the communication of love's enlightening truth to each person according to the reality of his or her situation; and, recalling the words of Christ to the Samaritan woman, He did not say that she had not been married, but that the man with whom she lived, at that moment, was not her husband: 'he whom you now have is not your husband' (Jn 4: 18). On the one hand, then, there is the objective truth to be discerned through the external forum of the Church; and, on the other hand, there is the word of God's enlightenment of our present reality: love's truthful discernment

[108] Paragraph 9: Cardinal Ratzinger, Congregation for the Doctrine of the Faith, http://www.vatican.va/roman_curia/congregations/cfaith/documents/rc_con_cfaith_doc_14091994_rec-holy-comm-by-divorced_en.html.

of “today”. Thus, while it looks as if the love of the law is inflexible and crucifies us, it is the law of love that we pass from death to life; indeed, the inflexibility of the law is, truly, the inflexibility of the truth, but the law of love transforms what would destroy us into what rebuilds us. In other words, natural truth can indicate the reality within us; but, at the same time, it is inadequate to bring about the conversion it implies; and, therefore, while truth crucifies us, the word of God brings about the utterly impossible passage from death to life[109]. But this is a supernatural work of God and, as such, is the fruit of either a direct gift of God or the preaching that plants faith (cf. Rom 10: 14-17) and puts us in movement: either one of the many movements in the Church[110] or the movement of the Church Herself.

Given that without Christ we can do nothing (cf. Jn 15: 5), we need a rediscovery of a relationship to His word and His Church. If "Ignorance of the Scriptures, is ignorance of Christ" (St. Jerome, quoted in Dei Verbum, 25), and if 'it is only in the mystery of the Word made flesh that the mystery of man truly becomes clear' (*Gaudium et Spes*, 22), then "ignorance of the Scriptures" is ignorance of man. Conversely, not only is knowledge of the Scriptures knowledge of man "in Christ", but knowledge of the Scriptures enlightens us in the light of eternity.

But we cannot walk alone and, therefore, I encourage you in

---

[109] Cf. Pope Francis, “Pope’s Morning Homily: Pastors Should Accept the 1st Step, Let God Do the Rest”, December 15th, 2016: https://zenit.org/articles/popes-morning-homily-pastors-should-accept-the-1st-step-let-god-do-the-rest/. Although, in reality, the first step is also a work of God; however, it may not become clear that this is the case until later.

[110] Eg. *The Neocatechumenal Way, Focolare, Communio et Liberatione*, Youth 2000 etc.

whatever way to find a people with whom to share the path of life; for, in the end, whatever we experience of the help of God is not just for ourselves but for our neighbours too (cf. Jn 4: 39-42)[111].

Part II: On Christ's Love of the Sinner

"On the Truth that Heals (cf. Jn 8: 31-32) the Crisis of Marriage": The more Precise Question

Introduction to Chapter 4: Part II: On Love's Truth[112]. Do we believe that God can act in our lives; indeed, that God can act for the benefit of everyone in our lives? In the myriad situations of life, God is not a "situationist": God alone is the one who acts for the good of everybody in everybody's life; and, therefore, the intricate difficulties that we all experience when it comes to our concrete history are a call to faith: faith in God the Good Shepherd. In other words, there is not a difficulty, not a complex history, not a trail of sin and its harm that is beyond the actual help of God. On the one hand, then, let us acknowledge the reality of our lives; and, on the other hand, let us appeal to God for help.

---

[111] *If you would like to discover, further, how the word of God has helped me in a variety of ways, please read the following work: http://www.hprweb.com/2015/02/witness-begets-witnesses/). But for a book length investigation go to* Scripture: A Unique Word, *2014, particularly Chapter 2 for the perspective on the conversion of a man and; finally, for further work, go to the trilogy:* From Truth and truth, *2016 (the books are all published by Cambridge Scholars Publishing: Newcastle upon Tyne).*

[112] Fr. David Meconi has now taken this piece for publication in May, 2018, on the Homiletic and Pastoral Review website: http://www.hprweb.com/author/francis-etheredge/.

God knows the concrete facts of our lives, the tangle of relationships and the number of our children; and, what is more, God knows the longing for love which He expressed in each one of us. Let us not be afraid, then, to turn back to the Creator: to the one who is truly creative in addressing our whole human needs.

In the course of the on-going discussion of what is possible for the remarried within the embracing love of the Church there is emerging a number of distinct aspects: accompaniment as a "way" of drawing people closer to the Church (I); a "moment" of discernment in that process in which a couple recognise the need for abstinence and the possibility of being helped to do this (II); and, thirdly, a philosophical point in Pope Francis' Letter On Communication which may impact on our understanding of the Christian life: particularly on our conversion to reality (III).

What does it mean to accompany the "remarried"?

There are three related questions to consider here: The first question is: What does it mean to remarry? (Ia). Then there is the further question: Is there a real possibility of a true death of a marriage? (Ib). Finally: What is accompaniment? (Ic).

What Does it Mean to Remarry?

In this context, "remarriage" means that a spouse has "married again" when the husband or wife from the first marriage is still living. If the Church has recognised that the first marriage was invalid, then the couple are free to "remarry"; for, in this instance, there is no prior, valid marriage. C. S. Lewis, it seems, reasoned that if Joy Gresham was married to a man who was divorced, the fact that he was divorced invalidated his marriage to Joy; and, therefore, Jack Lewis and Joy Gresham were free to marry. This reasoning, while not identical to the Catholic practice of discerning the validity of a marriage, nevertheless indicates the kind of facts that can illuminate a particular situation. "Remarriage" here, then, is specifically concerned with those whom the Church has not, for one reason or another, recognised as being free to marry; and, therefore, there remains a prior act of marriage awaiting the discernment of the Church. This discernment is necessary because Christ Himself says that those whom God unites man cannot separate: 'What therefore God has joined together, let not man put asunder' (Mk 10: 9; cf. Mt 19: 6). In other words, the sacrament of marriage is an act of God that the Church cannot undo; but, in the mission of love to which she is called, she can seek to identify if, in fact, God has acted and a sacramental marriage does in fact exist.

The embrace of the Church is in the discernment of whether or not God has acted; and, if He has, then this cannot be undone. Christ does not say to the woman at the well that she was not married but that she was not married to the man with whom she now lived (cf. Jn 4: 18). The first part of the process of accompaniment is, then, an act of love towards the "remarried"; and, in reality, entails an act of evangelising enlightenment. In other words, it is not just about understanding that a previous marriage has existed, it is also about seeking to understand the presence of God in the history of people who are now drawing closer to the Church and, indeed, encouraging them to draw ever closer. At the same time, the Church's vocation is to help us to see that the act of God that brings a marriage to exist is irrevocable.

Just as the act of God that brings a human being to exist cannot be undone, neither can the act of God which brings marriage to exist be undone. Even more, however, must it be said, that God continues to act in the history of each of us; and, therefore, it is not as if the reality of marriage is God's last word in our salvation history. In other words, it is how to respond to the call of Christ to conversion that transforms a preoccupation with law into a proclamation of love[113]: to turn away from ourselves and towards Him; and, therefore, the goal of accompaniment is to participate as fully as possible in the Gospel of Love: both evangelizing and being evangelized!

Can a Marriage Die?

Carla Mae Streeter, OP, has summarised an argument which runs as follows: just as when the "bread" of the Eucharist dissolves and Christ is no longer present, so the death of a marriage is when 'the human love dissolves ... [such that] the matter of the sacrament in that case ceases'[114].

Although it seems plausible to argue for the "dissolution or death" of a marriage, this does not take account of what God has

---

[113] Cf. Cardinal Wuerl, "Is it confusion or different approaches", http://cardinalsblog.adw.org/2017/01/confusion-different-approaches/?utm_source=linkedIn&utm_medium=social&utm_campaign=SocialWarfare; and cf. too,

Sandro Magister, "Buenos Aires and Rome. For Francis, These Are the Model Dioceses",

http://chiesa.espresso.repubblica.it/articolo/1351383?eng=y.

[114] "Reflections On Some Responses to Francis' *Amoris Laetitia*", ITEST Bulletin, Vol. 47 - #4, p. 9.

rooted in the sacramental reality of a temporal relationship in Christ: a temporal relationship in Christ which is also an image of the spousal banquet of eternal life. In other words, the Son of God's Incarnation founded, irrevocably, the Paschal Mystery, His death and Resurrection and Ascension into heaven, so His "relationship" to us established the possibility of our relationship to God and to each other. Thus the truth of marriage is that it is an irrevocably temporal "relationship" between a man and a woman, in Christ, established by God. If, then, the marriage was an act of God, in virtue of the very communion between man and God in Jesus Christ, then the "matter" of the sacrament is the reality of the relationship to which the man and the woman, on marrying, have entered into. In other words, just as an act of God is irrevocable, so is the "taking up" into that act all that pertains to it; and, therefore, just as the bread and wine is "irrevocably" the body and blood of Jesus Christ, after consecration, so is the human and the divine act of marriage indissolubly "one" in the sacrament of marriage.

Whatever a marriage suffers, then, in terms of the temporal reality of disappointment, betrayal, uncertainty, doubt and sin, the whole sacramental reality of marriage is the whole Paschal Mystery: the irrevocable "mission" through which Christ brings the new life of the resurrection out of the whole existential situation of the marriage (cf. Jn 2: 1-11).

What is Accompaniment?[115]

To bring a person to Christ or to stand in the way? What are these two possibilities from the point of view of grace?

The first possibility is a discernment, by the Church, of the work of God. What is the action of God in the concrete situation of a person's life[116]? This act of discernment is not a human invention. To see what God is doing in a person's life, we might say, is a central act of the mission of the Church. The Church is a body and, therefore, there is a participation in what the Lord is doing: a participation which begins with drawing close enough to "see" what the Lord is doing in a particular person's life; and, in view of the nature of the Church as communion, this participation is an inseparable part of the work and mission of the Lord. The Lord calls us into communion, not abstractly but, to begin with, in and from the actual reality of our lives; but, at the same time, the call to communion has an inherent conversion in it: a concrete

---

[115] This section was first posted as a response to an article, and the discussion of it, on the following website:

http://www.hprweb.com/2017/05/chapter-eight-of-the-post-synodal-apostolic-exhortation-amoris-laetitia/#comments. The article itself was by Cardinal Francesco Coccopalmerio, entitled "Chapter Eight of the Post-Synodal Apostolic Exhortation, *Amoris Laetitia*, translated by Andrew Guernsey.

[116] Subsequent to inserting this section, the following article has been published: 'Divorce, Remarriage, and "Discerning the Body"', by Dr. Matthew J. Ramage: http://www.hprweb.com/2017/05/divorce-remarriage-and-discerning-the-body/. On the one hand, I agree that there is an objective nature to sin. On the other hand, there are degrees of subjective participation in that objective reality: from diminished responsibility to consent to the malice of the act. It is an integral part of the work of an accompanying discernment to identity the reality of sin in a person's life and, if possible, to help that person to respond to Christ's call to conversion.

turning to the Lord.

What, then, does it mean to stand in the way of an action of God? Perhaps, concretely, to stand in the way of the Lord's call to communion is to overlook the help that Christ has given to me, which may be a part of the help which the Lord wants to give to another; and, therefore, instead of sharing how the Lord has helped me, I may be unwilling to reveal the humbling reality of my own life, its many falls and the many times that the Lord has shown me that He exists, almost, to help.

The gift of faith, I increasingly think, is an expression of the Lord's mercy: it is an act of God's mercy to be called to faith – to believe that God exists and that He acts to help. The call to faith, then, is already, in its way, the beginning of the act of mercy which matures unto eternal life in the communion of saints[117].

In the "moment" of discernment that abstinence is necessary

It has also become clear that there can be a "moment" when two people recognise that, in reality, the Word of God, the Tradition of the Church and the voice of the Magisterium (cf. Dei Verbum, 10) has enlightened them to see that they are called to renounce being "remarried" and to live as brother and sister. In this situation there is a power of love that makes possible the fulfilment of a word as dramatic as the woman caught in adultery

---

[117] Without knowing the program personally, the National Catholic Register reported on the "Archdiocese of Detroit Begins Building the Marriage Catechumenate", by Peter Jesserer Smith: 'http://www.ncregister.com/daily-news/archdiocese-of-detroit-begins-building-the-marriage-catechumenate.

experienced when Christ said to her: "Has no one condemned you?" .... "Neither do I condemn you; go, and do not sin again" (Jn 8: 10-11). The fact that Christ said He did not 'condemn' the woman is evidence, precisely, of what Pope Francis is seeking to accomplish: a love that expresses reconciliation with Christ. In other words, there is a moment in which God is experienced as the One who delivers from sin[118] and its slavery.

At the same time, 'Cardinal Müller, while prefect of the Congregation for the Doctrine of the Faith, ... said that the divorced and remarried cannot take Communion, except possibly when they try to live "in complete continence"'[119]. Objectively, then, there is a distinction between coming closer to the Church, perhaps not realizing the reality which is lived, and beginning to perceive that God has called us to live "in complete continence". In other words, in the situation of God calling people to live "in complete continence", there is already a recognition of the evangelical goal: of living the truth in love; and, therefore, it is in this situation that Cardinal Müller says that there can be recourse to the sacraments of 'Communion' and, by implication, Penance. In other words, there is no confusion here about the reality of conversion: God has begun to initiate the call to complete continence; but, in terms of the daily work of transforming "remarriage" into a relationship akin to that of being brother and

118 Cf. Francis Etheredge, Witness "Begets" Witnesses, http://www.hprweb.com/2015/02/witness-begets-witnesses/.

119 Staff Reporter, "Cardinal Müller: Communion for the remarried is against God's law", http://www.catholicherald.co.uk/news/2017/02/01/cardinal-muller-communion-for-the-remarried-is-against-gods-law/.

sister, there is a change which is both dramatic and graced. How, in actual fact, God brings about the grace of conversion is, indeed, a challenge to us to understand; but, nevertheless, if the Church in Her wisdom recognizes that this is indeed a favorable moment to receive the sacraments of Penance and Communion, then this is because of striving to live "in complete continence"[120].

In the concrete circumstances in which people find themselves, both in the course of their enlightenment and following it, there is a new reality to embrace: a new action of God to "be birthed". Thus the sacraments are not, here, a substitute for change but are, in good faith, an expression of it. In my experience[121], however, there is the possibility of a kind of "sacramental treadmill" of sin and absolution; and, indeed, there came a "moment" when I was sick of returning to my own vomit (cf. Proverbs 26: 11). God answered my despair and "planted" faith: Just as God can bring creation out of nothing so He can bring new life to the sinner (cf. *Catechism of the Catholic Church*, 298[122]). I cannot endorse

---

[120] At the same time, however, there is a very instructive piece by Cardinal Paul Cordes, "Spiritual Communion: Freed from the Dust of Centuries": 'Then, I remembered a possible way to relate to Christ which might be open to remarried and divorced persons. For centuries, it was known to be the believer's comfort and nourishment for unity with God: *spiritual communion*. Spiritual communion is tied only to the interior desires of the heart' (http://www.hprweb.com/2016/12/spiritual-communion-freed-from-the-dust-of-centuries/). In other words, spiritual communion is a person's intense, personal prayer to the Christ in the Blessed Sacrament. Similarly, there is a general need to "reclaim" the power of the word of God to help us. Who knows the mind of the Lord and how He will respond to the heart of those who turn to Him?

[121] Cf. "Accompaniment: On the Truth that Heals (Part I)", https://www.linkedin.com/pulse/accompaniment-truth-heals-francis-etheredge?published=u.

[122] Francis Etheredge, Witness "Begets" Witnesses,

enough, then, the wisdom of a journey of accompaniment that is especially relevant to helping this encounter with the Lord to be a profound deliverance from the slavery of sin to the freedom of love.

I am inclined to believe, then, through my own bitter and protracted experience of recourse to Christ's sacraments and His Church, that there is an abiding wisdom in the renewed realism concerning conversion and how to assist it. At this level, then, pastoral action which is rooted in *Amoris Laetitia* does seem to possess a realistic welcome of the sinner.

Is there a philosophical point in Pope Francis' Letter on Communication which may help us to understand the Christian life: particularly conversion to reality: 'In and of itself, reality has no one clear meaning'[123]? (III: Part One on Communication and Part Two on Ambiguity)

III: Part One on Communication. Pope Francis says: 'In and of itself, reality has no one clear meaning' and, in the next sentence, 'Everything depends on the way we look at things, on the lens we use to view them'[124].

On the one hand, then, it could be claimed that this is philosophically flawed in so far as it suggests that there is no

---

http://www.hprweb.com/2015/02/witness-begets-witnesses/.

123 "Message of His Holiness Pope Francis for the 51st World Communications Day", 24th January, 2017, https://w2.vatican.va/content/francesco/en/messages/communications/documents/papa-francesco_20170124_messaggio-comunicazioni-sociali.html.

124 Pope Francis, "World Communications Day", 24th January, 2017.

objective reality: that 'In and of itself, reality has no one clear meaning.' Indeed, it could be argued, this statement opens up the possibility that a 'lens', whether Christian or otherwise, is some kind of arbitrary imposition of meaning which, in a way, could just as well be one lens among many and not, intrinsically, more relevant, useful or truthful than another. In other words, is this a "bald" statement of a philosophical position that makes it possible to advance the view, mistakenly, that the interpretation of human experience has no roots in reality itself and is, as it were, an imposition or "labelling" of meaning that does not "reach" or recognize what really exists?

On the other hand, however, if we take this statement in the context of "World Communication Day" it could be argued that, according to the "take" of journalists, commentators, experts, politicians and people generally, that there is in fact a "variable" meaning that would lead us to conclude: 'In and of itself, reality has no one clear meaning.' Or, alternatively, we might argue that just as there are scientific, embryological, psychological, philosophical and theological insights into the beginning of human personhood that, in fact, we need the complementarity of the different disciplines to enrich each other and to enable, through a wealth of study, to go beyond the limitations of any one account. At the same time, it could be maintained, there is an abundance of evidence in the "hearing of the Word of God" that it can speak to us in a nuance that is at once personal to us, available to others in so far as we share it and, therefore, it expresses a range of meaning that is extraordinarily subtle and able to address each one of us in our daily reality. In other words, it is possible to maintain that there is a legitimate sense in which it can be said that 'In and of itself, reality has no one clear meaning.'

Part Two on Ambiguity. If the first part of this section has considered taking a single statement two ways, one positive and one negative, is it possible that "ambiguity"[125] has a "good" about it - the good of causing us to search our hearts?

What if God, who allowed the suffering of Joseph in view of the good he had planned to bring about (cf. Gn 50: 20), has allowed a certain ambiguity in the expression of Church teaching in view of a good that arises out of the challenge to which it calls us: the challenge to self-examination? Just as God did not move Joseph's brothers to harm him, yet He drew a great good out of it for His people, so God did not "engineer" an ambiguity in a Church document but yet intends it to be a great good. In other words, if we believe that the Spirit of God is at work in the Church, is there a good that exceeds the human reasons of an ambiguous expression in Church teaching?[126] Could it be, in a sense, like Christ challenging us with an unfamiliar use of language in order, as it were, to scrutinize our attitudes and reactions the better to purge it of an unhelpful perfectionism: a kind of literal Catholicism that makes us more conscious of a deviation than of the person who needs help.

It is true, then, that the grace of God brings about the

[125] The original stimulus for this section was an article by Fr. Regis Scanlon, OFMCAP, "The Flawed Strategy Behind *Amoris Laetitia*" (http://www.hprweb.com/2017/08/the-flawed-strategy-behind-amoris-laetitia/) and my response to it at: http://www.hprweb.com/2017/08/the-flawed-strategy-behind-amoris-laetitia/#comments (September 8, 2017).

[126] Cf. Fr. Regis Scanlon, OFMCAP, "The Flawed Strategy Behind *Amoris Laetitia*".

fulfillment of the law of love; but, in so doing, perhaps God needs to bring about a greater good of helping us to respond to the sinner He is seeking to save. Perhaps the problem to be faced is not so much the fear of transgressing a moral norm, real though this is, as that people who are living through this transgression need us to have a wisdom that exceeds observing the problem of "their" transgression. In other words, it is not so much that people are "objectively" at fault, as that they need help to recognize the discrepancy between their "subjective" understanding of what they are doing and an objectivity, not just of the moral law in general, but of their real situation. When Christ says to the woman caught in adultery, "go; and sin no more", it is clear that He has both objectively expressed the truth about adultery and the freedom that that the woman needs from sin (Jn 8: 3-11).

Perhaps, then, what the Spirit of Truth seeks from us is not so much a grasp of the unchangeable law, as that we need to see the blindness of the blind in order to help them; and, in order to see the blindness of the blind, we need to see the blind spot in our own vision. The blind spot, then, is the whole situation in which, in this day and age, people "wake up" to find themselves, for a whole variety of reasons, in complex situations which exceed their power to resolve. The truth, then, that sets people free (cf. Jn 8: 32) comes with a powerful gentleness (cf. *Dignitatis Humanae*, 2-3) that needs, in its human exponents, all the subtlety of understanding and help that grace makes possible. There can never be a truth that contradicts truth – but there can be a lovelessness which contradicts the loving expression of the truth: 'St Teresa Benedicta of the Cross says to us all: Do not accept anything as the truth if it lacks love. And do not accept anything as love which lacks truth! One without the other becomes a destructive lie'[127].

What if, then, part of the problem of the "reception" of Pope Francis is precisely his emphasis on the actual reality of the human personhood and life of the sinner[128]. While not rejecting the clarity of the principled expression of the truth, perhaps Pope Francis is seeking to imitate Christ "scandalously": that in the reality of the moment of being discovered to be a sinner there is one who does not condemn us but utters a transforming word of life: "go, and do not sin again" (Jn 8: 11). Are we not called to do likewise?

Part III: "Being Open to Life": "Abstract Norm" or "Embodied Word"?

Introduction to Chapter 4: Part III: "Abstract Norm" or "Embodied Word"?[129] This is probably one of the more difficult parts of the book as it engages more deeply with the contemporary questions concerning the meaning of Christian Marriage.

---

[127] Homily of St. John Paul II for the Canonization of Edith Stein, Sunday, 11th October, 1998: 8.

[128] Cf. Cardinal Francesco Coccopalmerio, translated by Andrew Guernsey, Chapter Eight of the Post-Synodal Apostolic Exhortation, *Amoris Laetitia*: 'Pope Francis evaluates reality through the person or, again, he puts the person first, and thereby he evaluates reality. What counts is the person, the rest comes as a logical consequence' at http://www.hprweb.com/2017/05/chapter-eight-of-the-post-synodal-apostolic-exhortation-amoris-laetitia/.

[129] Fr. David Meconi has now taken this piece for publication in the Winter of 2017, on the Homiletic and Pastoral Review website: http://www.hprweb.com/author/francis-etheredge/.

Nevertheless, given that the book as a whole has drawn upon real experience and what it teaches us about the human person, so the philosophy, theology and spirituality of these pages is very much how, actually, we exist and love.

Preamble

We have a temptation to separate a moral norm from its existential reality and, in so doing, to imagine that we have "an abstract norm"[130] instead of an "embodied bioethical word". In the very transposition of the concrete, incarnate, bioethical word of "being open to life" to an abstract norm, being open to life, is no longer an expression of the whole human being in whom it is to be found. On the one hand, then, a "moral norm" can be abstracted from the whole human being of which it is an integral part and, in the process, it becomes a "moral principle" without root or natural expression in human being; and, on the other hand, even when "being open to life" is recognised to be an integral expression of human being, it is necessary to recognise that it points beyond the virtue of integral truth to the requirement of the help of God to live it. In other words, "being open to life", while an intelligible expression of the mystery of human personhood, intrinsically requires the full truth of the human person to be liveable: the full truth being that God makes possible what is impossible to human

130 *Although the expression, 'abstract norm' (http://www.ncregister.com/blog/edward-pentin/moral-theologian-tampering-with-humanae-vitae-could-cause-untold-damage), is in current usage, the use of it in this essay is more about contrasting it with an 'embodied word' than with a precise account of how others are using it.*

beings (cf. Lk 1: 37). It is possible, then, to think of a moral norm as if it were an "external" imposition, a kind of rein on human behaviour which, unless exercised, results in a certain kind of wildness: as if virtue is an imposition of what is, as it were, an unnaturally external restraint; and, if we do, we are in danger of imagining that moral norms exist "independently" of actual human beings: real human people and their relationships.

Alternatively, if an action is described as 'intrinsically wrong' can it lead to a 'black and white'[131] understanding of human morality: as if understanding an action to be 'intrinsically wrong' necessarily leads to an insensitivity to the subtleties of conscience expressed in lived human lives. On the one hand, it is possible to be insensitive to the actual reality of transgressing a moral norm, the elements that disguise, mitigate or impoverish human responsibility; and, therefore, it is always necessary to be able to listen to the actual reality of a human person, as lived in a concrete act, to determine how to help him or her to live the fullness of human personhood to which we are all called. On the other hand, acknowledging the concrete circumstances of an actual human act does not "dissolve" the reality of human personhood which is either fulfilled or frustrated in human action. In other words, while the recognition of human culpability admits of many degrees and complexities, the reality of human being is what, in itself, determines an action to be what it is. Thus, even if, in a particular case, there are factors which mitigate against a person understanding the harm that he or she is doing, there is

[131] *Cf. https://www.lifesitenews.com/news/francis-praises-prominent-humanae-vitae-dissenter-for-his-radical-new-moral.*

nevertheless an objective truth of the human person which explains, ultimately, the nature of a human action as harmful or beneficial to the human being.

What, then, is the Church's expression of "being open to life"? (Part I). What is the reality that this teaching is seeking to communicate? (Part II). What makes the help of God necessary to living the full truth of human marriage (Part III).

"Being open to life" in the teaching of the Church

There are many expressions in the teaching of the Church which help us to see that the Holy Spirit has guided her to grasp what God has brought about in the creation of the human being: the human being who is a "being-in-relationship": in relationship to God and to others: a relationship in which morality is as integral to fellowship as communication is to communion. In what follows, then, there is a brief collation of a number of ways that the Church has begun to elucidate the word God has embodied in the one flesh of married life (cf. Mt 19).

Glimpsing the Whole of Human Being

"Being open to life" is integral to the whole of marriage: 'any use whatever of marriage must retain its natural potential to procreate human life' (*Humanae Vitae*, 11).

'This particular doctrine ... is based on the inseparable connection, established by God, which man on his own initiative may not break, between the unitive significance and the procreative significance which are both inherent to the marriage act' (12). Thus, in the context of the whole document, Blessed Paul VI is elucidating an understanding of the integral nature of the human person: that husband and wife are ministers 'of the design established by the Creator' (13)[132].

The doctrine of *Humanae Vitae* exists in the context, however, of the renewed understanding of marriage as biblically and personalistically expressed in the Second Vatican Council: 'The intimate partnership of married life and love has been established by the Creator and qualified by His laws, and is rooted in the conjugal covenant of irrevocable personal consent' (*Gaudium et Spes*, 48). Thus there is the triple emphasis on what is 'established by the Creator', biblically understood as a 'conjugal covenant' and entails each person's 'irrevocable personal consent'. Moreover,

---

[132] "Being open to life" does not imply that every marital act will bring about the conception of a child (11). But because being open to life is inseparable from spousal love, being open to life does imply that there will be no use of 'force' in marriage nor can a spouse deliberately 'impair .... the design established by the Creator' (13).

More fully, Blessed Pope Paul VI wrote, in *Humanae Vitae*, of love as 'fully human, a compound of sense and spirit'; of 'a love which is total – that very special form of personal friendship in which husband and wife generously share everything .... [and] loves that partner for their own sake, content to be able to enrich the other with the gift of himself'; of a 'married love' that 'is faithful and exclusive of all other, this until death' (9). At the same time, 'responsible parenthood' takes account of 'biological processes involved', 'innate drives and emotions' and 'expresses the domination which reason and will must exert over them' and, moreover, attends to 'relevant physical, economic, psychological and social conditions', all of which is brought to perfection by a 'right conscience' interpreting the 'objective moral order established by God' (10). Furthermore, 'The Church ... in urging men to the observance of the precepts of the natural law ... teaches as absolutely required that any use whatever of marriage must retain its natural potential to procreate human life' (11).

understanding the truth of the human person can be further understood to take account of the wholeness of human being in the following ways. On the one hand 'The total physical self-giving would be a lie if it were not the sign and fruit of a total personal self-giving, in which the whole person, including the temporal dimension, is present: if the person were to withhold something or reserve the possibility of deciding otherwise in the future, by this very fact he or she would not be giving totally' (*Familiaris Consortio*, 11); and, on the other hand, the whole human being is to be understood as 'the person himself in the unity of soul and body, in the unity of his spiritual and biological inclinations and of all the other specific characteristics necessary for the pursuit of his end' (*Veritatis Splendor*, 48; but cf. also *Familiaris Consortio*, 11).

The point, then, of this summary of the teaching of the Church is that it indicates, within the limits of these expressions, that there is a whole human reality, one in body and soul (*Gaudium et Spes*, 14), which communicates what is 'established by the Creator' (*Gaudium et Spes*, 48). St. John Paul II goes on to say that 'Womanhood and manhood are complementary not only from the physical and psychological points of view, but also from the ontological. It is only through the duality of the "masculine" and the "feminine" that the "human" finds full realization' (Letter to Women, 7); and that this relationship is 'a relational "uni-duality", which enables each to experience their interpersonal and reciprocal relationship as a gift which enriches and which confers responsibility' (8).

Part B: What is the Reality that this Teaching is Seeking to Communicate?

The horizon entailed in the gift of fertility 'entails a certain "openness" to the "gift" of a child from the Author of life; and, in view of that very uncertainty, indicates a "natural" attitude of "gratitude" for the "gift" of a child (cf. Gn 4: 1). Furthermore, even if 'there are reasonable grounds for spacing births' (*Humanae Vitae*, 16), the very psycho-spiritual attitude "inscribed" in the marital act disposes the spouses to accept an "unplanned" gift of another child. Thus there is a "pro-life attitude" which is inseparable to the marital act; indeed, it is as if the pro-life attitude and spousal action are the "inward" and "outward" expression of love'[133].

If we follow the direction of these observations, they lead us to considering the unity-in-diversity of law: law that integrally embodies love and expresses the mystery of the Creator's personal communion in the one flesh of marriage.

What, then, is the unity-in-diversity of law? On the one hand it is possible to think of law as an invention of human beings, an imposition on what exists and an obstruction to freedom; but, on the other hand, the law of gravity is "embodied" in the relationship between big and small objects. In other words, the law of gravity is not an imposition on what exists, it actually arises out of what exists. Just as the laws of the universe exist to be discovered, so

---

133 Volume I-Faithful Reason (of the trilogy *From Truth and truth*), Lady Stephenson Library (Newcastle upon Tyne: Cambridge Scholars Publishing, 2016), p. 176.

discovering the laws of nature does not "cause" them to exist. What is more, without the law of gravity, it would not be possible to do many things; indeed, it is as if the very "relationships" between different sizes and types of matter is a kind of "framework" for the activity of each day: a kind of "parable" about the law of God providing a framework for the flourishing of human beings. But, just as what exists becomes conscious in human beings, so the universal laws of nature are "personalised" in the natural law: the law we draw upon to express reason's recognition of the enduring reality of what exists[134].

Similarly, the internal structure of the human person exists in itself; but, through the process of investigation, it is possible to recognise that the internal structure both exists and exists as a uniquely personal expression of the whole human being. In the internal structure of the human being there is what regulates growth, development, digestion, recreation and work; and, as we act according to the needs of hunger, warmth and rest, so we help the natural processes that contribute to our day. Although, in general, it is possible to recognise that these processes are regulated and that their activity is usually unconscious, there is nevertheless a "coming into consciousness" of what is otherwise ongoing and helpful; and, indeed, our conscious participation in what is otherwise unconsciously regulated brings about the ingredients which, as it were, sustain us in our daily lives and help us to recognise what needs to be remedied or addressed.

Psychologically, too, as the human being's biological

---

[134] Cf. A much more extended discussion of this on the basis of texts from both St. John Paul II and St. Thomas Aquinas: Chapter Three of *Volume I-Faithful Reason*, 2016.

development unfolds, so the implicit processes of thinking, feeling, willing, communicating and doing develop and unfold; and, incrementally, just as the child begins to walk and to talk, so the relationship between parents and child is stimulated and challenged to become conscious and articulate. Conversely, where there is a repression of experience and our reactions to it, so there is a corresponding frustration of human development and relationships. In other words, there are internal psychic principles which, like the biological and physical expressions of human activity, are a part of the dynamic development of human beings-in-relationship.

When, then, it comes to marriage and the outward expression of a love determined to be lived in spousal communion, the whole individuality of being a man and a woman enters into a dynamic whole, bringing with it all the ingredients of being male and female; and, therefore, the dynamic of married love arises out of the reciprocal self-gift of each to the other in the fullness of being husband and wife. The spirituality of love, drawing upon its psycho-physical structure, makes the spouses conscious of an attitude that fulfils the act of marriage: an attitude that is inscribed in the very self-giving of spousal love and is expressed in the embrace of love being open to life – even if there is no possibility of the transmission of life. In other words, inscribed within the very dynamic and dialogue of marriage is the willingness, if the celebration of marriage is begun, to cooperate in what will bring the spouses so indescribably close and, simultaneously, leave open the possibility of the transmission of life.

Thus, just as there is, as it were, an outward coming together in the celebration of marriage, so there is an interior attitude which seeks the fulfilment of the other in the utter gift of oneself. Integral, then, to the reciprocal gift of self is being open to the transmission of life as an inseparable expression of being wholly given to the other and being wholly received by the other. In other words, deeply within the dynamic of loving, is the mystery of life from love: that from the gift of self arises the possibility of the gift of a child; and, even if that possibility bears within it the trace of uncertainty, this helps to dispose the spouses to see the child as a gift: a gift in the receiving just as spousal love is a gift in the giving. This "embodied word of gift", both expressing an interior psycho-spiritual attitude to the reciprocal gift of spousal love, is itself a gift of the Creator and expresses, uniquely, the eternal giving at the heart of the Blessed Trinity.

What Makes the Help of God Indispensable to Living the Full Truth of Marriage?

To begin with, then, we cannot really understand the "one flesh" of marriage if we do not read the indications which point us to the inner life and Being of the Blessed Trinity. In other words, ultimately, the "one flesh" of marriage expresses the personal reality of man, male and female, being "one being" in the mystery of communicating life through the action of the Creator; and, as such, God has manifested in the flesh an expression of the mystery of His own Being: At once a singular and a dynamically fruitful communion. Thus, in the end, the only credible explanation of man, male and female, forming the fruitful communion of marriage is that this expresses the interpersonal reality of the

Blessed Trinity. On the one hand God is the uniquely singular Being; and, on the other hand, there are three persons in one God. Thus God is both uniquely personal and each Person is, as it were, open to the life of the Other: an interpersonal communion that is also a kind of mystery of "person from person".

The law, as it were, of the inseparability of the 'unitive significance and the procreative significance' (*Humanae Vitae*, 12) of the marriage act is Love's self-expression in the flesh of human marriage. In other words, the very "relational being" of the Blessed Trinity is "translated" into the one flesh of marriage as an "incarnate" expression of the "reality" of the Blessed Trinity. Just, then, as the first man and the first woman were created in relationship to God, so God anticipated, through this, the coming of Christ and His Church. It is not as if, then, the origin of man, male and female, is "independent" of the whole of salvation history; rather, the spiritual significance of Adam from the ground and Eve from the side of Adam, is a kind of threefold sign: it looks "back" into the mystery of "person" from "person" in the Blessed Trinity; it looks into the depths of human personhood and embraces "difference", "complementarity" and "fruitfulness"; and it looks forward to the manifestation of Christ and the Church.

It is clear, then, that if the ultimate explanation of marriage is the mystery of the Blessed Trinity, then just as the inner-life of the Blessed Trinity is its origin and ground, so the very life of the Blessed Trinity is expressed in the Sacrament of Marriage. Living the gift of marriage, then, is not only living an inseparable communion of being one flesh it is, too, living the vocation of marriage out of the life of the Blessed Trinity; indeed, in a certain sense, the whole sacramentality of marriage is lived as if the life of the Blessed Trinity is lived in us. Grace, then, is not some kind of "oil", "grease" or "fuel"; it is, as it were, the life of God lived in us: the life that God lives in us makes living the gift of marriage and family life possible.

In Conclusion

Finally, then, being open to life is an "embodied ethical word"; it is the word of the Creator enfleshed in human being and realised in marriage. Being open to life, then, needs the whole Christian life like the mystery of the Blessed Trinity needs the whole reality of being God to be lived. Just, then, as being open to life cannot be understood without reference to the whole of reality, neither can it be abstracted from the whole of human reality if it is to be intelligibly understood as an embodied word of lived love enfleshed in human marriage. Furthermore, just as marriage exists in the context of the whole of salvation history, so it benefits from the call to conversion (cf. *Humanae Vitae*, 29): the graced call which enacts in us the fulfilment of the promised covenant of love to which God calls us.

It is impossible, however, to "abstract" our lives from the history of salvation and, therefore, God finds us where we are and takes us where we cannot go[135]. At the same time, however, as He

[135] This is my reading of the pastoral love expressed in *Amoris Laetitia*; cf also *The Human Person: A Bioethical Word* (St. Louis, MO: En Route Books and Media, 2017), pp. 23-24. Nevertheless, I am aware of the controversy that surrounds this document, particularly around the theme of an intrinsically wrong action (cf. *Correctio filialis:*
http://www.correctiofilialis.org/wp-content/uploads/2017/08/Correctio-filialis_English_1.pdf). At the same time, however, I note that in Pope Francis'

seeks to establish in us the gift of becoming what we cannot be without Him (cf. Jn 15: 5), God progresses the revelation in human history that began at Creation and will unfold until the end of time: the revelation that human being, in all its fullness, cannot be understood except in the light of God (cf. *Gaudium et Spes*, 36); and, therefore, there is a "word of God" embodied in human being which is as stable, enduring and ever open to a deeper understanding as the mystery of God Himself being the Blessed Trinity.

In the end, then, precepts, if they are a true expression of embodied love, cannot be understood except in relation to the fullness of human life (cf. Jn 15: 1-11; cf. Jn 10: 10) that manifests the fullness of human being; and, furthermore, the validity of a precept derives from the embodied word of God and not from the process through which we come to appreciate and to understand

---

letter to Archbishop Paglia, Pope Francis says: 'It is clear that not adopting, or else suspending, disproportionate measures, means avoiding overzealous treatment; from an ethical standpoint, it is completely different from euthanasia, which is always wrong, in that the intent of euthanasia is to end life and cause death' (Reported by Jim Fair, November 16th, 2017: https://zenit.org/articles/pope-francis-addresses-end-of-life-issues/). In other words, Pope Francis recognizes an intrinsically wrong action: 'euthanasia, which is always wrong, in that the intent of euthanasia is to end life and cause death.'

But, in that truth cannot contradict truth, it is necessary to recognise what is valid even if, in the process, it challenges us to renew our hold on what we know to be true. In a word, addressing people in the plight of an incomplete grasp of their subjective reality does not invalidate the goal of objective truth to which God's love calls us; indeed, it is precisely to bring about the goal of conversion that we are addressed "where we are": that God can bring us to where, without Him, we cannot go. In view of this call to conversion, I remind the reader how helpful it was to be refused confession when I was considering marriage in a registry office; and, therefore, there is a value in "no" that is perhaps underestimated.

it. Although, it has to be said, the process through which we come to appreciate and to understand the fullness of God's gift to us is an intimate part of the way that God brings us, together with others, to the fullness of truth.

There is an embodied word, then, that the Creator has expressed in the act of creation: a word which is discernible to reason and evident in Revelation; and, therefore, even if there is a subjective inability, blindness or the possibility of misreading it, the objectivity of the act of God has established this word as an intrinsic part of His dialogue with each and every one of us. Even in view, then, of the pastoral challenge of how to communicate the truth established by God in creation, to a generation that is probably very shrouded in uncertainty, is a very real need to be addressed; but, in the process, there does remain the "goal" of knowing reality, and ourselves as a part of it, in a way which preserves the possibility of coming to the full truth to which we are all called.

Ultimately, then, it may be necessary to admit that reason needs faith to be itself in order for it to be open to the full truth of human being; and, if reason needs faith, then faith needs to be itself too and to be formed from the gift of preaching, Revelation, witness, conversion and the sacramental life of the Church. This faith, that God can make the barren fruitful (cf. Gn 15: 1-6), that God can pass through closed doors (cf. Jn 20: 19-23), that God can make a history of salvation out of a history of sin, is the faith of Abraham, Mary and the Church[136] in the Paschal Mystery of Christ's death, resurrection and sending of the Holy Spirit.

---

[136] Cf. *Catechism of the Catholic Church*, (CCC), 142-149 etc.

In the experience which follows we can see how God acts in the very concrete reality of our encounter with others in the name of Jesus Christ.

Alan Soares

My name is Alan Soares and I am 52 years old. I was born in Kenya, of Goan parents and emigrated to England with my family in 1972 at the age of 7. I grew up in a Catholic family, in east London, but moved to Cheltenham after getting married. I have been married for 22 years to my wife Daniela and we have six children. I am self-employed and volunteer at Cheltenham General Hospital and the local Sue Ryder Hospice, as part of the spiritual care team.

Alan Soares (and Frank): Evangelization and the Help to the Family

Sunday 23rd July 2017

We arrived to stay the first night with a family from Guardian Angels parish, whom my companion Frank has known for more than 30 years. When we arrived we were greeted with great joy, and it soon became apparent that our visit and further stay was an answer to fervent prayer.

It turns out that the mother of the family had been close to breaking point, and had spent much of the previous day weeping and on her knees in prayer to the Virgin Mary and Saint Mary Magdalen (whose feast day it was). She had been asking the Lord for help with her youngest daughter with whom she had terrible rows for the whole of the past week, and suddenly she received a call asking if some brothers beginning the 2x2 mission could come to stay for a night. Hence she greeted us as 'angels' who had been sent by the Lord.

I was initially very reluctant to stay beyond the first night, as I wanted to experience some of the hardship and graces to which we were all called at the beginning of the 'sending out' convivance. In truth I was also keen not to be seen as taking the 'easy way out' when we returned. Frank however, was adamant that the mission was first for this family, who had been experiencing all sorts of difficulties. He correctly saw it as providential that he had been picked out to go to this area. In order to remain in communion with him I eventually agreed to stay, and as the week progressed and events unfolded I realised that he had been right.

We ended the first evening by doing evening prayer with the whole family who spoke very openly and humbly of their difficulties, judgements and lack of communion during the previous week. It was evident that the Lord's peace really had descended upon the household. It was also remarkable that the parents were the ministers of the Word for a community at Mile End where we hope our eldest son will walk whilst he studies at Queen Mary.

Monday 24th July

We visited Holy Family church in Dagenham for a communion service which was led by a newly ordained deacon. He preached an excellent sermon and gave a lovely blessing to a young man from the parish who attended mass on his 15th birthday. He obviously had a great gift for caring for the youth in his parish. Afterwards we introduced ourselves and explained the mission and were about to leave when a lady, who was the parish priest's secretary, said 'Stop! You must stay for some refreshment or you might shake the dust from your shoes!' We assured her that we would never do such a thing, but she said she had heard the previous week's gospel about the sending of the 72 and remembered it. Over tea and chocolate we talked for over an hour and a half with deacon Rick and a couple of other parishioners, one of whom said the parish could do with all the missionaries it could get. It turns out that the deacon had family in the Way back in the U.S and he had met many of the seminarians from the house of formation at Allen Hall. He had great regard for Fr. Francesco Donega, who was one of his lecturers. The parish priest had gone to Lourdes together with Bishop Alan Williams and over 250 young people from the diocese. I gave him my experience of growing up in Brentwood diocese, of going on similar youth trips, being on a spiritual high, but then being left with no follow up, of drifting away from the Church and falling into sin. He said that the youth were 'being failed' and agreed that it was vital that they had the continuing help and support. As we were leaving, the deacon pressed us to accept some money, which we finally accepted on the condition that we gave it to the poor. He gave us a wonderful blessing in front of the Blessed sacrament

We then went to pray over the town of Dagenham. The highest point was a tower block near the tube station, but had a keypad controlled entry system on the ground floor of a shopping arcade, so we couldn't get in. Whilst resting on a bench outside we caught sight of a poor man who headed into the arcade. We tried to follow him to give him the money we had received earlier but he seemed to vanish amongst the crowds. On our way out we were walking past the entrance to the tower block, when some residents were on their way out and held the door open for us! We went to the top floor with a great view over the whole town and Frank said the prayer with great force and conviction.

We then went to the parish of St. Vincent's and met an Indian priest who was covering for the parish priest who had just retired. He seemed very sceptical at first and thought we were trying to get something from him, but when we asked for a blessing and gave him the money we had for the orphanage he ran in India he was really stunned and followed us down the road as we left, urging us to come back to Mass another day and meet the parishioners.

The day finished with a visit to the sister of the mother of our host family, whom she had urged us to visit if at all possible. This lady had been in the Way since the earliest years at Guardian Angels, but had left 17 years ago after a serious argument with a priest after a pilgrimage. Since then her health and her life had spiralled downwards. We found her in a very dark enclosed house very near to St. Vincent's. She was delighted to see Frank, being an old family friend, and welcomed us in. She told us all her troubles and listened to Frank's experience. She then asked to hear my experience and was stunned to hear of so many parallels in our lives. Most importantly, she was really heartened to hear of how God had acted in my life when He gave me the grace to accept and embrace the cross of loneliness which I had for so many years in my life. She too had been a poet and songwriter and saw how God had specifically chosen the people to visit her. Her whole mood and demeanour completely changed as we prayed with her and took a Gospel by chance, and really spoke the truth to her. She said she still listened to songs from the Way every day, and there seemed to be real healing of all those years since she had been away. Frank and I saw clearly how the Lord had not forgotten this sister, and his great love for her. She urged us to stay for supper, so we stayed and encouraged her for a couple of hours.

We returned exhausted to our home base, with Frank (aged 76) hardly able to walk. Somehow a large thorn had found its way into his shoe and caused a large blister.

Tuesday 25th July

After a very peaceful morning prayer with our host family we set off for Romford. The first priest we met was not interested but then we met Fr. Adrian, at Christ the Eternal High Priest. He was driving up back from his holiday as we were leaving. Initially hesitant, he immediately asked us come in when we asked for a cup of water. He gave us the run of his kitchen but said he was too busy to talk to us. After a sandwich and tea, we asked for a blessing as we were about to leave. This really seemed to change his disposition. He was also very happy when we asked where we could find the poor in his wealthy parish.

We next met Fr. Tom, the parish priest of St. Edward the Confessor. He was elderly and sick, hobbling about on two sticks. Initially a bit suspicious, he softened when we said that Bishop Alan had been written to about the mission, and gave us the Bishop's secretary's number so we could possibly get an appointment to see him on his return from Lourdes. He told us of his many health problems and sincerely asked us for our prayers when he has a major operation on the 16th of August. He gave us a blessing and tried to give us money which we didn't accept. He was unable to talk further as he had a young parishioner and her baby waiting to see him.

From there we had two profound meetings with the poor in Romford town centre. First we met Jim, an elderly dishevelled alcoholic, who seemed surprised that we wanted to sit and rest on the same bench as him. He seemed delighted that we were interested in his life and for some personal human contact. He told us his life story with great humour and his eyes recovered their shine. A lot of passersby seemed puzzled and taken aback by the attention this broken old man was receiving. As we were leaving he shook our hands, really grateful for the time we spent just talking with him.

Next we met Stephen and Lorraine, a couple who had been living on the streets for two years. As we walked past they called us over. After explaining our mission, and how we were 'homeless' for the week, they warmed to us even more. They both had terrible histories of drug and alcohol abuse and some strange ideas about Christ, which we were able to lovingly correct. We prayed with Stephen who was Catholic and used to be an altar boy, and he took a Gospel over which he seemed to ponder really deeply. After announcing the love of God for them we left.

Frank was adamant we should then visit my mother who lives in nearby Seven Kings. Again I was extremely reluctant, wanting to be seen well by the catechists. She had been really stressed about my welfare upon hearing about the mission from my wife, and so was shocked and delighted to see us turn up on her doorstep. She couldn't believe that of all the places in the country to which I could have been sent, I came to Brentwood diocese. She was happy and at peace and kept saying 'Look how God provides!'. We also went to visit my aunt and cousin who live just next door to her. I see how God sent us to my cousin in particular, who hasn't practised the faith for decades. She was fascinated and intrigued by the precariousness of the mission. It seemed to awaken a lot of questions about faith in her.

By this stage Frank could hardly walk anymore as his shoes were broken. I remembered that my brother had left a pair of running shoes at my mum's house. Providentially they were exactly the size that Frank needed!

Wednesday 26th July

We went to morning mass at St. Cedd's, my old parish church for 23 years. We met a brother from Guardians Angels parish by chance. As we were talking to him we were approached by a parishioner who asked if we were more of those people who were on a mission. She had met the three sisters of the other team to visit this diocese earlier in the week. Taken aback that her fellow parishioner was also a member of a community at Mile End, she wanted to know all about it. She said she wanted to know more as we, and the sisters she had previously met, seemed 'so free'.

After the highs of the previous day we came down to earth, walking for miles and miles to visit four far flung parishes where none of the priests were in, being in Lourdes with the diocesan pilgrimage. Determined to suffer a little and earn our stripes, we decided to return to Romford and sleep outside with the poor of the town that night. Waiting exhausted at the bus stop, we met a man called Mr. Ellis. He said he used to be a lecturer but since retiring he had lost purpose in his life. His wife had left him, and his two successful sons hardly saw him. Each day he just sat at the bus stop on his own, watching the buses and people come and go. It wasn't until we left him after 15 minutes when our bus arrived that we noticed the half bottle of whisky he was hiding by his side.

Once in Romford we scoured the town to find some poor people, but found not one in any of the places they had been before. A little dejected we returned to base and realised that we had been blind to the real mission of that day - Mr. Ellis whom we had left behind in our efforts to be a little 'heroic'. We knew then that God didn't want us to somehow try to earn his love or grace, but to have hearts and eyes open to see people who were suffering all around us. On my camp bed that night, and every other night of the mission, I really thanked the Lord for his love and mercy to me a sinner and prayed earnestly for all the brothers and sisters who didn't have a roof over their head.

Thursday 27th July

We visited another member of our host families relations - the sister-in-law, who was in desperate need of a word of encouragement. This lady too had been in the community at Guardian Angels many years ago, together with her husband, but both had left. They had subsequently got divorced when her husband left her and the children for another woman. She was now hurt and alone for many years and had stopped going even to the local church, not seeing the need for it as she could pray alone.

She was very defensive to begin with, but I remembered that our catechist Lorenzo said the most important and powerful thing was to announce the Kerygma. It brought me to tears when he said how in the moment it is announced, Christ stands at the right side of his Father in heaven and shows him his glorious wounds, winning for that person immense graces. This is exactly what I announced to this lady and all her defences fell before the love of God. She completely changed her position and said she needed to go back to church, and go with her children too. She received a gospel and seemed transformed.

Friday 28th July

The most important day.

We began the day at Mass at English Martyrs in Hornchurch. We met the dynamic parish priest who was from India. It was the most beautiful church we visited, but was in danger of being closed down in an amalgamation by the diocese. The priest listened really well and was interested in the Way, but felt he didn't have the time to commit as he was involved in so many other things in the parish and deanery, such as the RCIA, being the diocesan interfaith representative, and charismatic renewal etc.. He noted however, that so many of the groups within his parish were disconnected from each other along ethnic or national lines. He was really impressed when we gave our experience of life in the community with so many people who are so different. He said he would definitely raise the possibility of the Way at the next deanery meeting. He felt that the church in England was very conservative in nature. He was also an expert in mental health, from a Catholic point of view which was really relevant, as both I and our host family had people we knew who could really benefit from his help. He ended by giving us, and all the members of the Way in this land, a beautiful blessing.

Next we went to Upminster and met a wonderful old priest called Fr. Martin. He was a retired priest from Brentwood diocese, who now lived on his own in Cork in Ireland. He was often called back to cover for priests when they were away. He gave a very profound and insightful view of the crisis of the church in Ireland. After giving us food and drink he gave us a wonderful blessing with the laying on of hands. He also insisted on giving us money, which we said would go to the poor. It was also providential meeting him, because a sister from our community had gone to live in Cork a few years ago with her young family, and we wondered if this priest may be able to do a service for the communities there, instead of remaining isolated in his mother's old house.

Lastly, and perhaps most importantly, we went to Grays, way out in south Essex. Outside the train station I noticed what seemed to be an old lady, called Loraine. I asked her if she knew the way to St. Thomas' which she said was a ten minute walk away. After giving us directions she ambled off but then suddenly stopped and volunteered to take us there. I offered to carry her shopping bag, for which she was extremely grateful, as she said she was really unwell. She told us how this had been the first time she had set foot out of her house in ten weeks, that she had had a terrible fall at home and had lost all confidence. She had only come out to see the doctor for more antidepressants and had lost weight down to barely six stone. Shortly after, a very angry looking woman came along and nearly knocked her off her feet. Apparently this stranger had done similar things on other occasions for some unknown reason. Lorraine, though terribly shaken, said she was happy we were with her when it happened as she didn't feel as angry and upset as she had done before. When we arrived at the church she was going to leave us, but I had the inspiration to ask her how much further away she lived and if we could carry her bag home for her. Frank also said we could say a prayer with her and give her a word of scripture for her life. Very happy she agreed to do this. When we arrived at her home a further 15 minute walk away she invited us in, sensing in some way that we were no threat to her. She gave us refreshments and listened intently as Frank opened the Gospel for her. She received the word of the true disciple, who founds his life on the rock. After helping her to break the word a little and praying together, she said she had something very important to tell us which she had not shared with anyone else. She said she was only 62 but spoke of the many difficulties in her life and said that she had felt she couldn't carry on. She confided in us that a few days before she had written her suicide note. The only thing that stopped her doing something desperate that day, was seeing the beauty of the flowers in her garden and how some birds came to sing at her patio window. Still, on the Monday and Tuesday of this week she had spent the whole day saying out loud 'There is no God!'. She couldn't believe that on her first day out in ten weeks she had met us, who came to announce the love of God for her. She also said that she felt 'attacked', believing that an evil presence had been in her house. I assured her that we brought the peace of Christ with us, so she said at last she could sleep. She clung onto us as we left and we encouraged her to go to a church where she felt the presence of God, and assured her of our prayers for her.

On our way home we passed through Hornchurch. An alcoholic on a bench asked us for a pound. Used to not having any money we instinctively replied we had nothing. He then said 'Help me please I'm desperate.' Frank suddenly remembered the twenty pounds Fr. Martin had given us the previous day, so he emptied his pockets and gave it to him. The poor man seemed shocked and tried to give some money back to us, but we refused saying that God had sent us for people like him. At this he burst into tears, and Frank said the aspect of his face changed from that of a broken old man to one of a young boy. We hugged him and told him by name that God loved him.

Saturday 29th July

At the beginning of the convivance we had met Brian, a brother from the 1st community of Guardian Angels, who lives in Tilbury. Really excited that we were going to visit his home town, he urged us to see his wife Marylyn and their children if possible. Frank suggested we went there for lunch before visiting the church there, and yet again I wasn't keen on what appeared to be a social visit to one of the brothers. As events unfolded I found myself wrong yet again.

After this very pleasant lunch we went to visit the priest at Our Lady Star of the Sea, but he wasn't in, nor were the Sisters of Mercy at the nearby convent, whom Marylyn knew well. After travelling so far (it was the furthest church on our list), we decided to persevere and return later. Here the Lord used our interest in history to delay us! We visited Tilbury Fort, the site where Queen Elizabeth I had given her famous speech to rouse her navy to defeat the Spanish Armada. I had often wondered why the Armada had failed, but it struck me there that God didn't want to restore the Catholic faith to England with violence and war, but with mercy and love, such as on this mission.

Returning to the church we found the parish priest in and he directed us to the convent. Here we were greeted very suspiciously to begin with, when the nun who opened the door said "We don't need converting here!' When we said we knew Brian and Marylyn however, she immediately invited us in. Over lashings of tea and cake, three nuns listened to us intently and told us some of their histories. Despite being elderly, they were pin-sharp and very discerning about the church in the diocese. As we were about to go to visit one of the parishes in South Ockendon which we had missed earlier in the week, the Superior said she would call ahead by telephone. The parish priest agreed to see us at 7.15 pm, which left plenty of time. On leaving she asked for our prayers for their dwindling order and even gave me her own umbrella against the rain.

Back at the rail station we were dismayed to learn of huge delays on the line. When we finally got our train, both Frank and I fell asleep and got off at the wrong stop. By now we were late and had a further wait and long walk ahead. Frank thought it best to borrow a phone from someone and cancel the appointment with the priest, instead of arriving at least an hour late. Also, he was really tired and his feet were killing him. I suggested that maybe everything was going so wrong because the evil one didn't want us to go there. Frank thought I was going a bit over the top and we nearly had an argument. All of a sudden however, he changed his mind and said 'Lets go!'. Sure enough we eventually arrived over an hour late. After getting no response at the door for quite a while, we were about to leave dejectedly, when the parish priest appeared at a bedroom window. He asked if we were the two people the sisters had spoken of and then reassured, let us in. As we explained the mission and gave our experience he listened really well, noting however that we had arrived with sandals on our feet and a haversack! He showed us great hospitality and even offered to cook a meal for us. He is a fairly young, dynamic priest really keen to be involved in everything in his parish, and bring new life to it. He knew nothing of the Way, so we gave him a very brief history. At the end he said he wanted to be led by the Spirit. When he asked for some printed material regarding the catechesis, I thought to send him a copy of the statutes the Way had been officially granted by the Vatican, and maybe an initiator's book, by Kiko Arguello, as an introduction. He said he had no doubt we were authentic, because the Sisters of Mercy had vouched for us. Before leaving he gave us probably the most amazing blessing of the week, lasting almost five minutes! He also emptied his fridge into a large carrier bag and apologised for his lack of hospitality.

Here I saw the amazing way the Lord works. If we had not visited Marylyn, the Sisters of Mercy would not have welcomed us, and if we had not seen them they would not have recommended us to Fr. Francis, who in turn said he would not have received us. So much for my moralism! Other things struck us after our visit to this 'last' parish. It is dedicated to 'The Holy Cross', which is the feast of Frank's birthday - 14th September. I remembered what really struck me at the sending out convivance was when another of the national catechists Mauritzia, spoke of the cross, and that some of us were yet to truly embrace it even after all these years in the Way. Blessing God we returned to base, really full of joy.

Sunday 30th July

For the final day of the mission I had a burning desire to go Brentwood to the cathedral, in the hope of meeting Bishop Alan who had been away for most of the week in Lourdes. Unfortunately, we had missed him by just a day, but the priest in charge gave us a blessing and invited us to stay for the 11.30am Mass. As a young person I had always wanted to go to the Mother Church of my diocese but had never made it, so for me this was a bit of a pilgrimage. The church itself is beautiful, reordered and bathed in light. It was a joy that there was a baptism at that particular mass, so we were all able to renew our baptismal vows. Bearing in mind all the wonders we had seen in the week I was able to do this with faith and great content. It meant as much to me as when I had renewed my vows at the River Jordan at the end of the Way, after nearly 30 years of formation. During the eucharist we prayed earnestly for Bishop Alan, for all the priests and religious of the diocese and all the poor and suffering we had met. I couldn't help hoping that the little child we saw receiving baptism was a figure of a new community being born, perhaps in South Ockendon, if God willed. On leaving, I asked the priest to convey our warmest regards to Bishop Alan, which he promised to do.

We returned to our host family to complete a very late lauds and were struck by how the youngest daughter said that our week with them had been 'holy' and such a contrast to the week before. It was evident that a great peace and communion had been restored and that deep-seated issues were being addressed and healed. After lunch, Frank took the opportunity to speak seriously to the eldest son of the family who was visiting, who had left the Way and no longer attended church. This young man listened very intently to what we had to say, and accepted a Gospel by chance, saying he needed to really ponder what it meant for his life. Having a partner and a child of his own now, he knew he needed God's help and guidance.

Personal reflection

I arrived at the convivance quite destroyed, after a serious incident of sin I had committed in my family the week before. I felt really attacked by the evil one who kept putting into my mind that I was totally unworthy to even take the name of the Lord upon my lips. At the penitential celebration before we were sent out however, I was given courage to carry on by the priest, who said God could use even this, and my contrition, 'to be the engine of the evangelisation' for the week ahead. I see how much God loves sinners. How He can use even someone like me to reach other sinners who are just as weak and broken.

For me this was a week in which I saw miracles and which God sent me, in order to prove His existence to me and help me to have faith. I learned not to be such a moralist and to accept God's love, gratis. I see that this was a mission to family, both my own and to our host family and to their wider family, many of whom had left the Way but had not been forgotten by the Lord. I think it was not by chance that I was sent to the diocese in which I grew up and which is still in my heart.

We were astounded by the good will of so many strangers, who seemed to sense the presence of the Lord with us. Bus drivers went to extraordinary lengths to get us to our destinations, even stopping colleagues on other passing buses and instructing them to help us, without us even mentioning we were on mission. Train staff would leave their kiosks to direct us to local maps or go and print off maps without us asking. Staff in pubs and restaurants would never stop us using the facilities and customers would literally jump out of the way to give us preference! All this and much, much more for two Asian looking men in east London and Essex in this political climate was astounding.

It is an experience I will never forget, that has given me courage to face my cross and, with the grace of the Lord, to embrace it. I feel it was the beginning of the mission of the rest of my life.

Chapter Five

The Vocation to Write

General Introduction to Chapter 5: Writing a Way Forward. It has taken an interminably long time to get to the point of writing full-time; and, I am sure, a part of what has made the journey so long are all the courses, work and family demands which have been an inbuilt part of long-term daily life. Nevertheless, without this enormous experience of everyday life I would be a very different person and a very different writer; and, therefore, this is not about lamenting what did not happen but, rather, reflecting on what does happen: what the Lord in His wisdom is even now permitting to be possible. There is a line in one of the psalms which sums up, in a way, the possibilities of life which remain in the hands of the Lord to unfold, even in our later years: 'They still bring forth fruit in old age, they are ever full of sap and green,' (Ps 92: 14); and, what is more, that this fruitful old age is a sign of the presence of the Lord: 'to show that the Lord is upright; he is my rock, and there is no unrighteousness in him' (Ps 92: 15).

In one sense, then, this present season of writing arose after completing a book on the uniqueness of Scripture while still commuting to work; but, on beginning to write the second book, it became clear that there was too much material for one and therefore it became a trilogy on faith and reason. Thus, while there were other factors, it seemed as if the Lord was offering an opportunity to write. Then there was the disappointment of the very promising terms of the trilogy book contract realising nothing in the way of an income as the books did not sell in a way which helped us. Thus there has been a period of exploring other outlets with short articles, poems and a period of ongoing experimentation with business social media; but, again, while this generated some interest it has not automatically translated into commercial success. Nevertheless, though, all this experience has contributed to the "log", as it were, of the vocation of the writer and now constitutes a contribution to this final chapter on pilgrimage.

Pilgrimage, then, includes the whole life-long search for the vocational work which would both be fulfilling and contribute, as it can, to the search for truth which is so urgently needed in our times: a search which needs to investigate the foundations of human personhood in order the better to explain the nature of human action and the mystery of the human person as a "being-in-relation". At the same time, as these pages have indicated, writing is not about totally abstracting what is written from everyday life. There is a sense, therefore, that the thread of experience that has run through earlier work and is now increasingly evident in this one, is a part of the task of communicating more wholesomely the reality of conversion and its implications in the concrete facts of a particular life. Thirdly, though, the vocation of the writer is a vocation to communicate as widely as possible: to appeal to the everyday "person" concerning the profound crises of human identity and action which confront us "today". In a way, then, this book and this chapter are still about seeking the fulfilment of that vision and, at the same time, striving to meet the everyday needs of marriage and family life. In other words, the call to work is as alive today as it ever was; and, in so far as it continues to bear little financial fruit, so this work has to undergo changes that mature the vision while, at the same time, it engages more and more realistically with the task of providing a living that even in this late hour I still hope to contribute.

The pilgrimage of work, then, I hope will help to illuminate the choices that our children will make as they go into adult life.

This chapter is formed of three parts and charts, first through an earlier poem and piece of prose and a more recent prose poem (I), then later through a summary account of the most recent period of self-employment (II) and, finally, through a further reflection on writing itself, how the work of a writer is yet an on-going gift and task to be accepted and undertaken afresh (III).

Part I: Writing and Suffering

Introduction to Chapter 5: Part I: Writing and Suffering. This poem was written around 1995; and, in a certain sense, expresses that conflict between writing and being unable to write: between beginning, revising and being unable to complete a written piece of work. At the same time it expresses the challenge of a kind of naturalistic self-knowing and the growing realization that there are forces at work in our nature which originate in human prehistory; and, therefore, the invitation to self-knowledge, inscribed in self-development, needs a completing and complementing word which enlightens us from a far deeper and more mysterious origin: the origin of the word of God. Thus this poem expresses a kind of exhaustion: a health exhaustion certainly – but, more deeply, an exhaustion of the psychological explanations of life which, however adequate, are inadequate to express the fullness of life which exceeds them.

My Words Bled

Like a too fruitful sapling: unstoppable.
I wrote too much and exhausted
the body of the spring in which they ran.

I fled like a snail from its shell.

Prematurely leaving home, I neither left it nor could rest in it;
and not inhabiting its purpose made me homeless:
a disordered upgrowing in an ingrowing unhappiness.

Like a surgeon operating on his own stomach -
but not a surgeon nor with a scalpel -
only a loose mirror and a home-made knife.

I fell underground.
Lying in the silence, desperate to do nothing;
doing nothing I did what nothing can do:
listening in the damp muddy warmth

and breathing in the sight of a shepherd's lamp.

I visited myself in the company of others
and suffered their incision.
I wrote again:
far fewer words fell
like footsteps in the autumn;
or the first winged leaves
of an acorn
outbreaking a scabby compost.

Chapter Five: A "Day in the Life of a 37-year-old Student"

Introduction to Chapter 5: a "Day in the Life of a 37-year-old Student". This piece was published in 1994[137] and describes a time a few years before the end of the Life-Cycle poems of Chapter 1 and refers to the beginning of an abiding study of theology and philosophy, although it was often "marginalized" by the everyday needs of health, company and making ends meet. In one sense it was a time of "glowing", as if the beginning had begun and was not still to come, but in real terms there was yet to be the gift of knowing I needed the help of God: a turning point that turned me inside-out and showed the lie to striving to be a self-sufficient self-made man as "he" collapsed into the temptation to suicide.

There can be an outward conformity, in other words, to the "religious impulse" which is almost a disguise of the sinner within; and, indeed, it was the sinner within which needed to be seen and

---

137 *The Catholic Times*, p. 7, May 1st, 1994.

saved: a work which the truly saving God was in the process of accomplishing through the exhaustion of human effort, an ever elusive success and the ultimate poverty of an indefinitely prolonged project of self-development.

A Day in the Life of a Student

Sometimes morning is early and I resist it for a couple of hours longer; but usually I rise around six in the morning, rush a few exercises, a wash and shave, some breakfast if I have time – a meal for later if I am really organised – and I cycle off to the Cathedral to begin the day with Mass.

The "Colourings" of a Morning

Now that the daylight is seeping up the edge of the morning darkness, I lose the dense, tender winter blackness – still there, even if it is too cold to cry or too wet to notice – in exchange for this beautiful, calling blue.

I hope, when I arrive at the Cathedral, to find all the main lights off. For the glow of the red overhead electric heaters, suspended in front of an off-white-light, casts an outstretched swathe of fire-light from the open side of the Chapel into the grainy grey gloom that sits like a fog in the cavernous silence.

Dawn drops down like a waterfall through overhead shafts; but noiselessly, speaking a purply-hue.

I sit in the shade of all this and search out and share the longings of my heart with God.

Mass.

From then on the day can go several ways: seeking work to pay off the overdraft, the rent, the course fees; part-time decorating; trading my time for the possibility of paid work; Job Centres, interviews, letter and article writing – Thank God for the postman.

A visit to the bank manager becomes cold calling as I discover an in-house publication might consider an outside submission.

Frequently cooking, shopping, coming in and going out, bags full of everything in case the weather changes or I am out until late.

Always broke and dreaming of money, competition wins, schemes, individuals or organizations to write to, what else to sell, what I cannot buy and how to fill in "the hole in the wall".

"A deeper me"

An unbelievable but necessary amount of time strewn about in the process of breaking into regular work which is not a repetition of what I have done before but reflects, however obscurely, a deeper me, realised, in part, by the part-time correspondence degree in Divinity.

Afternoons turn into evenings, often in the library – especially if I have stolen some day-time conversations in the coffee shops – and a deadline is approaching or I want to escape the emptiness of a bed-sit a bit longer.

I research diet as a recreation. Four years of chronic fatigue compelled me to eat properly, undergo lots of inconclusive tests and satisfies, to some extent, my appetite for "domestic science". So I make notes on diet and experiment with food on a regular basis. How can I eat myself into a longer day?

Bed-time comes and with it prayer. But sometimes I doze off before I can complete it. I level out of a day lived until the end.

A "proper" job

But where, you ask, was the study? Somewhere, I will say, slipped in between everything else. And why do you not have a "proper" or a "regular part-time job"?

Because, I will say, living like flooding water once seduced me – but now I have stopped travelling, the water in the bowl has stopped swirling, and I can begin to see a reflection that I have striven almost all my adult years to find.

But, paradoxically, I cannot see myself in isolation from others and, therefore, I increasingly seek and benefit from the other.

Stability, friendship, expert and trained advisers are all necessary but insufficient. The Blessed Light of Divine Insight, like a yeast through the dough, must in His own time raise a recognizable identity. Patient I am not but perseverance I am given.

Sleep comes to take the incompletely me into tomorrow.

Part II: Meals

Introduction to Chapter 5: Part II: Meals. This is a theme which ranged right down the years and summed up, in a few lines, countless meals and moments that make up a life-time. The mood is again about movement: traversing the different states of life from estrangement to friendship, through to marriage and family life and all their "passing" or more enduring difficulties and joys.

At the same time as meals are like walking when it comes to relationships, an ordinary but absolutely necessary time together through all the difficulties and joys of sitting down at one table, meals are also ordinary and extraordinary: the extraordinary transformation of the bread and wine into the Body and Blood of Jesus Christ is both a communion with God and man and, in a sense, the goal of every simple prayer, meal and table conversation.

If meals are a measure of a healthily structured life, marriage and family life, then as you read this account you will see how this piece almost documents the correlation between conversion and the restoration of the routines that help our daily relationships to each other – not because a meal is a magical moment but because it is an "intense" moment of sharing all that we are as tired, grumpy, persevering, grateful and prayerful people.

Meals

We once eat together; but, with silence and disruption, eating
together fell into disuse.

Then there was a bowl of cornflakes between coming in and
going out.

Washing up in a hotel, plate upon plate of leftovers piling into a
bin beside an open mouth, discovered an unbelievable
"gaping" between what was unwanted and what was desperately
needed elsewhere.

Alone in a bedsit, in-between the family home and the possibility of marriage, never knowing if I would go back to the first or pass to the second; the room as cold as a fish-freezer, down by the river, especially on coming back from being away: a meal without a break from the solitariness of living is like being thirsty in the sea, eating salad without a dressing or meat without relish.

Cooking was an everlasting search for a dietary answer to health: a kind of experiment in the search for untraceable trace elements or the mysterious ingredients that almost never and only unpredictably alleviated the interminable tiredness.

Meals were mostly a useless generation of washing up and, after all the labour, gone too quickly and quietly.

Many meals were "like" family meals but were too temporary: a kind of pausing in the passing of busy days, wet days, walking days, wondering days, working days, days when company was possible, fake or genuinely open to the future.

Marriage was a new meal; eaten amidst the many guests and then alone together: a new beginning in an age-old practice of celebrating the action of God. Reading out loud and cooking, a particularly honeymoon moment, dining out as two in a quiet, little used restaurant in an almost empty place, only to change ceaselessly as the years brought boisterous children to the table.

Founding a family filled the table with flingers of bits hither and thither: mess and irritation; clearing up and the miracle of on-going patience and persistence. Meal by meal, the children grow and the games change, challenges come and go, strategies are varied, quarrels start and subside, protests are made and dialogue comes.

The phone goes in and out of pockets and places to hide, as if the washroom is a phone box or the kitchen a "doorway" to elsewhere and "switch off" an almost unintelligible notification of life next to you.

Sometimes a child is away and there is a gap at the table, almost a cavity, and a new dynamic arises, such as others find their voice and there are fireworks and noises and seat changes and a renewed perseverance to find conversations and moments of interest.

Then there are the longer absences, when first one then another goes away, returning still, but starting out all the same and coming back changed, different, with renewed histories and experience.

One meal, different to the rest, takes all the ingredients of our work and labour, failure and difficulties, passing us from giving up to going on, worn out to willing to welcome eight, if not ten children, falling after each other like a fountain that bubbled and burst open, two of whom went ahead to heaven. And when human strength failed, the hand of Christ stretched out to make possible walking on the water: the daily impossibility of managing to make ends meet, ill-health, study, training, work and the cherishing of a family culture.

Then there are many other meals, as on a pilgrimage or given freely, multiplied in the home or taken to other places, as with picnics, holiday travelling, gathering after a walk or on birthdays and anniversaries; and a number are every day and fraught with pre-meal panics, but readily eaten and a few are ridiculously elaborate and need a guest and a very few are monumental moments of being together in extraordinary places!

Meals are like bricks in a house, naturally opening out onto a meaning not wholly present: a family's planetary home; indeed, like stars, lights among billions, altogether lighting up the night sky, visibly pointing to communication between each of us and the word of God in the words of men (Dei Verbum, 13): a different kind of "breaking of bread", leading to communion.

Part III: Writing through the Setbacks

Introduction to Chapter 5: Part III: Writing through the Setbacks. While it is true that there are many ways to measure success, it is also true that one of them is the "bread and butter" money needed to provide for a family; and, so far, this lack of earned income has been more than elusive and, in that respect, a real challenge to faith: Is this whole writing project a final work of "ballooning" dreams or is it, in reality, the building of an investment that is yet to mature in terms of a family income?

In this penultimate passage of the pilgrim writer there is, then, a summary of the work which has been tried and, to varying degrees, has so far failed to produce "bread and butter".

Success is Steering through Setbacks

Success can include the publishing of long cherished but completely unprofitable work when it comes to generating an income! Success can also include writing published articles on profoundly essential, interesting and urgent questions. Success also entails generating a wide range of contacts and corresponding with collaborators; indeed, the enrichment of content is out of all proportion to the change of pace owing to working with others. Success is also about managing the transition from the "obstacle" that persecution presents to the "opportunity" that resignation realizes. Success is also about going from writing occasionally, in the course of work, on holiday, during a period of illness, in order to complete a course - to that on-going challenge to formulate experience in its fullness. Success is also about persevering in the face of failure, disappointment, the withering of wild expectations, the lack of replies and the tentative interest that turns into a tenacious unwillingness to take anything further. Success, then, is about discovering the way forward when almost everything is experienced as a setback.

In view, then, of a field of difficulties, there follows a brief reflection on five aspects of writing: the origin of writing (I); adapting to the hardships (II); the help of others (III); new ventures (IV); the on-going work (V).

The Origin and Nature of Writing-as-Work (I)

Writing both expresses the very process of an investigation and the challenge of communicating with another; indeed, in its psychological origin, the writer needed to write just as the rhythm of breathing includes exhaling as well as inhaling. In other words, following a profound resolution as a child to deny the painful humiliations of failing at school, writing became an essential method through which the past was reclaimed and reconnected with the present. Thus writing was a part of the process by which building dams as a child became dismantled as a young man even if, in the process of gradually recognising writing-as-work, there were many years of struggle, frustration and attempts at alternative employment. However, while it is true that writing is about articulating what is internal so that it is understandable to a person external to one's own situation, writing is also about bringing into existence a "work-in-progress": a vehicle of work.

Adapting to the Hardships (II)

While there are many advantages to writing regularly, the main one being that it is like being brought to pause, water in motion or a bird in flight, the daily schedule needs to take account of reading, news, exercise, regular meals and company. In view of being married and having a family it is also about accepting the shrunken budget and the promising contracts that did not, actually, produce anything other than the hard copies published. Thus there is the constant challenge to "invent" or "discover" a market, a way of writing, whether aphoristic or a series of short pieces, which takes a word like a leaf to places hitherto it has not lodged; and, in the process, nevertheless contributes to the real questions which need both investigation and dialogue and, at the same time, which progress the long term projects which are on-going to completion.

The Help of Others (III)

We begin as indebted to others, not only for an initial, progressive and advanced education, but also for that on-going encouragement, interest, proofreading, feedback and recognition which continues to make that debt grow; but, as it is a cultural debt, the only form of repayment is to contribute to the culture of the day: a culture which is always greater than the debris on the beach. In other words, the oceanic wealth from time immemorial, the breadth of input from the variety of subject disciplines and the characteristics of different kinds of cultural starting points, make for an immense "dialogue" of the peoples of the world; and, in addition, we are nevertheless "present" to a reality which, in being discovered in its truth, is always available to be recognised and "opened" further for the sake of the common good.

New Work Ventures (IV)

As a vehicle of work, it could be argued, writing responds to a wide variety of needs and opportunities; and, currently, includes the project of writing a "Top" Post: a piece that is both attractively written and capable of touching a number of "live" points of interest. The challenge for the "new" writer, without a current academic position, salary or research grant, is to find that fragrance which catches the breeze and draws all and sundry to the workshop: to the excitement of fashioning an unfamiliar but friendly account of what is in fact both naturally fascinating and a challenge to put into words. In many respects, writing is an instance of the very origin of thought, entailing as it does that initial articulation of what, in fact, is susceptible to a literary investigation; and, therefore, implies a certain relationship between what exists and the possibility of our investigation of it, which further suggests the following question: How can two so disparate entities, as writer and "subject", be so "closely" related?

The On-Going Work (V)

Writing from scratch, then, involves that on-going challenge to be a new colour in the crowd, another note on the air or a trace of scent that leads back to the freshly flowering "old rose" in the garden; and, as such, draws on an older mix of ideas, culture and activities, freshly enriched while, at the same time, putting forth new shoots with that ageless colour on an aging stem.

Who knows what will turn the occasional piece into a series, the aphoristic saying into a book, the book into a few lines or words into pounds, shillings and pence?

Part IV: The Pilgrim Writer

Introduction to Chapter 5: Part IV: The Pilgrim Writer. In one sense it is obvious that, having written about a variety of pilgrimages, writing and pilgrimages go together; but, in another sense, the vocation of the writer entails a pilgrimage: the perseverance that bears the traces of forty years of writing. Writing, once scrapped, because it was too painful to go on rewriting and endlessly expanding, became more disciplined in the course of numerous qualifications and, at the same time, began to leave a trail of different kinds of work, generally prose or poetry, such that themes began to emerge and to constitute the basis of a number of books.

Over the years, then, many other people have been a part of this pilgrimage of work; and, whether they have known it or not, walking a little or a long way along this path together has no doubt contributed to the fact I am still on the road.

There are three sections to this final piece on writing-as-pilgrimage: What is writing about? (I); Do we invent our own image or draw out the substance of our reality? (II); and, finally: What has this to do with the family on pilgrimage? (III)

What is writing about? (I)

There is scope for all kinds of experimental writing strategies - from the one sentence invitation to think through a basic question about human identity to the longer, perhaps popular or more studied piece on questions which propel us into the long haul: the investigation which takes us to further study. The challenge, then, is to enter this "sea" of interactions and to stimulate a "moment" of almost contradictory silence into which thoughts about life are able to seep without actually detracting from the business of the day. Indeed for you it might be that you have a meeting to go to, a deadline looming, a product to sell or a service to market. But for me it is about "opening" a thought so that the philosopher or theologian will be "started" into the most absorbing of searches: an account of the human person that does justice to the mystery of human being.

Where words are almost written "through" us, the vocation of the writer is to take flight on the expression of experience which is already "begotten" in us. But, alternatively, 'inherent in every being is its meaning: that "meaning" which is intelligibly present in it: that "word" or "idea" of the Creator'[138]. Thus there is both the work of articulating the reality of our experience and the work of expressing what we are as human beings: the gift and task of being able to explore and express our very nature! Writing receives what has been sown and develops it further; but, in addition, the writer hopes to open the many possibilities that lie dormant in a person's imagination. If a bird left an imprint in the snow and indirectly inspired Chinese calligraphy, what might you leave that could help another to discover a word waiting to be written? Even if the thoughts which run on have, as it were, outrun their origin, they retain the trace of having passed through an opening which made them possible. An author, therefore, enters a dialogue that, once begun, goes on endlessly; and the greatest hearts open upon visions which time can scarcely acquaint us with. In other words, even the very impulse of culture implies the possibility of an endless number of relationships each, as it were, entailing a new opening on an "Unbegotten" beginning: a new conversation with

[138] Francis Etheredge, *Volume I-Faithful Reason* (of the trilogy: Truth from truth) (Newcastle upon Tyne: Cambridge Scholars Publishing, 2016), p. 72.

the Creator and His creatures.

Inventing an explanation or actually making sense of our history (II)

I have written about the challenge of identifying the common thread that a history of work has revealed; and, in the process, draw upon three intertwined dimensions: conversion; the vocation to marriage; and the possibility of becoming a writer.

But was it an imposition on reality to seek themes out of a life so "impressionistically" lived? Perhaps human personhood is so plastic that work is not really a fundamental expression of each of us? It could be that each one of us "fills a gap" in a company, a project or a training program which, for what it is worth, was necessary at the time – but which does not lead, long-term, to a career path any more than a mixture of rubble can be built into an "amalgamation" of the different buildings from which it all came. In other words, too many discrepancies, changes of direction, diverse skills or elements of work, really add up to no-one-trade, profession or consistent activity. Or perhaps it is better to think of the rubble as providing a new opportunity for beginning a building which, while resembling a variety of previous structures, is actually a new work, prompted by the materials and reasons of the "moment". Thus it is not that all this history points to a particular "talent", like data indicating the presence of a planet that has hitherto not been clearly distinguished from the surrounding input of the sky, and brings with it a new focus or, better, brings into focus what actually exists; rather, it could be that this new configuration of the rubble is no more a closer approximation to the real me than melting plastic and claiming a significance for the shape it happens to make.

What if, on the other hand, even the new structure that arises out of the rubble does not just correspond, in various ways, to the "source" of each brick and item to be drawn upon, but that actually it really is about taking a working history as a whole and discovering, little by little, what it has revealed about the person whose trail, as it were, it really is? Thus, incomplete and inconclusive as it may be, each part of a working history is like an aspect of a whole; but, taken apart from that whole, it is like a piece of "broken" pottery which struggles to speak about either the work of a potter or the individual pot of which it is a fragment. In other words, perhaps it is not just about looking at the individual life as if it were a life-project that is completely the work of our own hands; indeed, it may be a part of the problem that we imagine that, in fact, we are the potter and not just the clay. Thus what looks to us as a mess and a-wandering all over the place may, in reality, be the indications that our life is being shaped rather more than we are the shaper.

Certainly, it has seemed to me, that I have tried over the years to go in so many different directions that, almost, it was about being a rudderless boat; but what if, on the contrary, these failures were more the like blows which, in the end, were knocking off pieces of rock that bring a sculpture to exist[139]. Perhaps, then, it is more about looking at this working history from the point of view of the presence and perception of "Another" and not just in terms of whether or not I accomplished this or that goal at one time or

139 An image that I know C. S. Lewis has used.

another. Perhaps, fundamentally, my mistake is to look at my life from the "inside" out and I need, through the reality of history, to glimpse the realisation that it is not just about discovering a particular identity as discovering that there is both an "inward" and an "outward" contribution to it: a combination of what has been working out from within as well as what there is, or "Who" even, has been bringing what was within to an expression which exceeds my own frustrated efforts. Indeed, it is possible to say that "God makes a path through dead ends".

What has this to do with the family on pilgrimage? (III)

Just as the Holy Family accompanies us, as it were, so we accompany each other: both in our own families and in whatever way the Lord makes possible.

Each part of our pilgrimage, then, is not isolated from the walk as a whole or from the culture in which we live; and, therefore, persevering in the search for a living as a writer immerses, in a way, my own family in this quest. Thus it involves my wife's willingness to bear with this daily-write, as it calls us to pray constantly for inspiration, guidance and all the practical implications of doing it; and, at the same time, the children can see how prayer impacts on us all and involves the question: What difference does prayer make to me earning a living? In other words, being open about the reality of work is not only humbling but it is also uplifting: it helps me to see that there is a trail of providences that evidences not only a path of work – but a vocational path that points to God acting in the field of work. Work is, it seems, a part of that whole which God envisaged when

He envisaged all of us as expressing the creativity He gave us (cf. Gn 1-2); and, therefore, if there is a purpose to writing and, more generally, writing about the Christian life, it is about bringing a "touch of human experience" to the study of theology[140].

A particular work

If writing, then, has focused me on the communicative power of words, it shows that communication arises out of our being-in-relationship[141]. But the very nature of reality as intelligible tells us, as it were, that the Creator has spoken a word through us: that each one of us expresses a radical uniqueness – wholly psychosomatic, integrally one and utterly differentiated in an identity which makes "relationship" an inseparable expression of our common humanity. Thus the work of a writer entails the work of addressing the people of our times: the people to whom it is necessary to reach so that together we may advance the wisdom of recognizing all who exist: each of us receives the gift of existence in a way which radically declares that each of us is a person-gift-in-relationship.

The family on pilgrimage, then, is not just "our families" – but the whole human family as it progresses through time and the

---

[140] Cf. Also Chapter 2 of *Scripture: A Unique Word*, 2014; and, for more on witness and pilgrimage, see Chapters 14 and 15 of *Volume III-Faith is Married Reason* (of the trilogy *From Truth and truth*, 2016): all of these books are published by Cambridge Scholars Publishing.

[141] Cf. Francis Etheredge, *The Human Person: A Bioethical Word* (St. Louis, MO: En Route Books and Media, 2017):

http://enroutebooksandmedia.com/bioethicalword/. The first two chapters of this book, too, draw heavily on the experience of the author.

times through which we are living. We are called, both through our own experience and because of the difficulties of the day, to be present and active; and, therefore, let us hope in the Lord of time that "today" is a day of hope and help to the families of the world.

In this final experience, it is clear that pilgrimage is also about questions that go to the depths of our faith; and, in going to the depths of our faith, these questions resound in the depths of each one of us.

Corinna Turner

Corinna Turner is a British Catholic author, Lay Dominican and occasional journalist. Her novel 'Liberation' was nominated for the Carnegie Medal Award 2016 and her books have also been placed in the Catholic Arts and Letters Award and the Catholic Press Awards. Her main published work is the 'I Am Margaret' series (Catholic dystopian novels for young adults and adults). Corinna has been writing since she was fourteen and likes strong protagonists with plenty of integrity. She was raised Methodist, migrated to the Anglicans, and finally swam the Tiber in 2010!

Corinna Turner: An Experience of Pilgrimage and Thoughts on Martyrdom

Stuck in the Dover traffic on the way to WYD 2016

The Dominican Youth Movement had a delayed start to the World Youth Day pilgrimage, but should still make it to Krakow ahead of Pope Francis

The Dominican Youth Movement pilgrimage to World Youth Day has got off to a fiery start – the pre-departure meal is too spicy to eat. Queue much glum staring at plates – but never mind, we plan to breakfast in Cologne, and eat dinner at Colditz Castle (now a youth hostel!).

At 10.30pm on Friday we set off... but by 12.30pm the coach is crawling and by 2am we have ground to a halt entirely. When the coach slowly comes awake again about four hours later the A20, six miles from Dover, resembles a huge car park.

Disembarking, we say a rosary, play games, and dance to a ukulele, witnessing and entertaining everyone else in equal measure, until at 7.30am – yes! – we pile back on board... drive a grand total of thirty metres... and stop again.

It's a very penitential one muesli bar each for breakfast and eventually, almost twelve hours after we came to a halt, a vehicle arrives with bottled water for the stranded traffic. God bless (belatedly!) the Dover authorities!

It's with a certain sense of the surreal, that we pull into Dover ferry terminal in time to catch the 2pm ferry – after almost 14 hours of queuing.

Apparently the delay, including the extraordinary five-and-a-half hours in which we failed to move at all, was caused by the presence of just one single French Passport Control officer at Dover, dutifully trying to check every passport.

But we're on the ferry at last and, after a most welcome meal in the restaurant, we feel quite surprised to find ourselves in France.

Alas, we won't now be visiting Cologne, or Colditz, but on the upside, it's all part of the adventure – and we should still be in

Krakow before Pope Francis!

The Journey Continues...

France at last! After our almost fourteen hour wait at Dover, the mood on the coach is joyful during the drive from Calais to Poland. But we pass a few things en route that prompt more sober reflection: the refugee camp at Calais, bright and cheerful in the glorious sunshine, but still a bleak sight; the signs for Dresden, about which no one can recall anything other than saturation bombing; and a large number of homeless sleeping out on mattresses as we pass through a German city: refugees, we wonder?

But after a total of 41 hours on the coach, we finally draw into Korbielow, a scenic mountain village near Poland's southern border. Here, amid pretty houses and utilitarian telephone poles - blame for the latter probably lying with the communists - is a similarly utilitarian youth hostel, with 4 combined shower/toilets for 40 people. Uh oh. But it also comes with forty actual... BEDS! Into which we fall with fervent thanksgiving! Well, after Sunday Mass in Polish...

The following day is our retreat day, so after a prayerful morning, we walk to Slovakia and back, crossing the border of a sixth country in three days.

In the morning it's back on the coach for the very scenic drive to Wadowice, where we will be staying for World Youth Day proper. Registration comes first, then we've barely eaten our pack lunches before we are whisked away to the homes of kindly Polish hosts, who promptly feed us a second - delicious - lunch.

Replete, we're soon back in John Paul II square in the centre of Wadowice enjoying the carnival atmosphere as pilgrims from all over the world prepare to watch the Opening Mass on the big screen.

At the end of which... World Youth Day 2016 has officially begun!

World Youth Day reminds us of the risks and rewards of our faith

Are young people from the West ready to fully embrace the dangers and delights of Catholicism?

The train door opened, revealing a man brandishing a very long, very sharp kitchen knife. For a moment I remained paralysed. Should I run away? But the... train steward? ...greeted me pleasantly, so I smiled back and went on my way as though my heart wasn't performing uncomfortable antics in my chest. Back in my seat, a member of my group said they'd seen the steward making sandwiches earlier. Knife explained; false alarm. But having just – belatedly – heard about the martyrdom of Fr Jacques in France, cooking wasn't the first thing that came to mind on a train, and this totally insignificant incident was actually, for me, a moment of profound challenge.

World Youth Days are always great schools of the virtues, especially patience. Queuing for meals, queuing for Confession, waiting for events... Annoyance or opportunity, it depends how you choose to take it. But I think after this summer of violence, there is a very particular challenge to every 2016 pilgrim, one which each accepted unconsciously when they took the decision to attend.

Still, with police cars at every junction of Kraków and army helicopters circling overhead, few European pilgrim won't have thought at least once, however briefly: if something happens here, just because we are Christians, are we willing to pay that price? (Let's not forget that for pilgrims from some parts of the world, attending WYD may be the safest thing they've done in ages...)

We were reminded at catechesis this morning that the early Christians spread the faith through the witness of their lives. But not only their lives: let us not forget that 'the blood of martyrs is the seed of Christians'. Can we not hope and pray that this new wave of martyrdoms might lead to the re-evangelisation of the West?[142]

---

[142] The first and third articles were first published on the *Catholic Herald Blog* (text provided by the author).

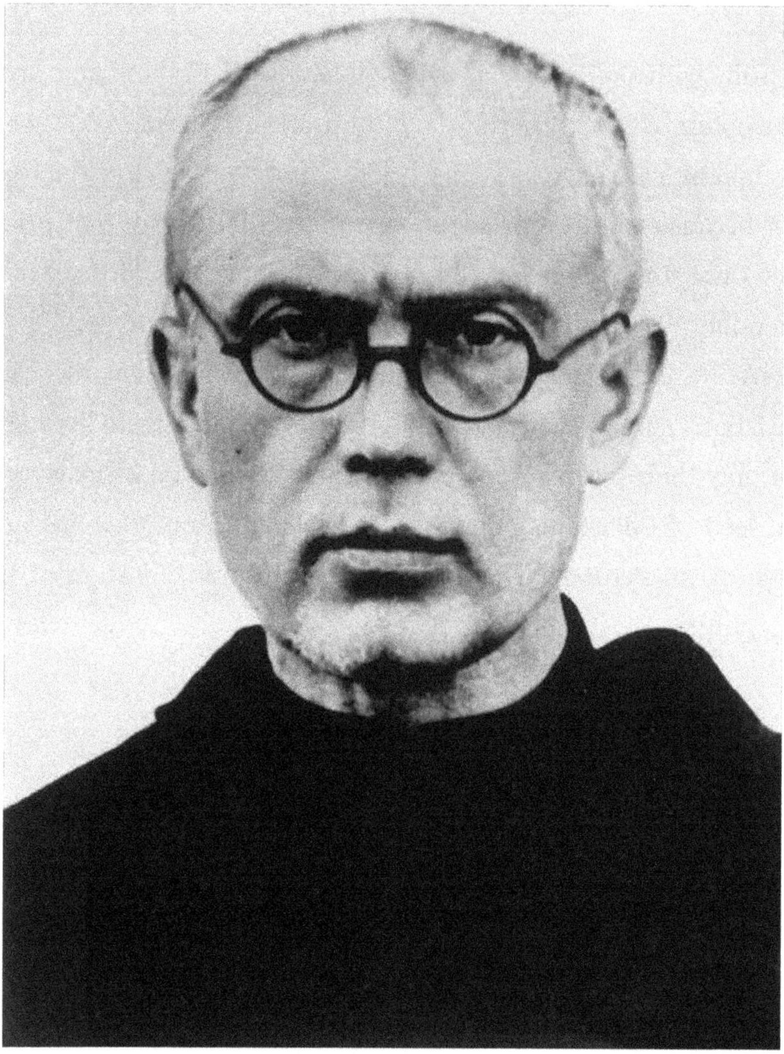

Saint Maximilian Kolbe, OFM Conv.

Courtesy of Wikipedia

Epilogue

As this book comes to close it is possible that there is no unifying theme, that the whole project is a willful conglomeration of disparate pieces or there is, as it were, an accidental connection between them but no common substance; or, on the contrary, what unites the whole work is the call to faith: that whether it is our health, passing faith to our children, going on pilgrimage as a family or as a part of a variety of groups or communities, the circumstances of our life or the difficulties of work – there is a common call to faith. The Christian Faith is not an abstract programme of truths that bears no relation to reality: as if Revelation was not received "through" the intricacies of human experience; rather, just as the word of God is steeped in the history of human action, so our lives are a constant opportunity for God to act in whatever way will bring the good we need. Just as the Creator envisaged all the vocational possibilities of human beings, including a generous openness to the gift of life, so Jesus Christ is The Good Shepherd whose word, ever spoken in whatever way it is, seeks us out to help and to encourage – making possible what is beyond us to do.

"Doing", however, does not necessarily mean achieving overnight success: the number one single, album or bestselling novel; rather, it may mean that we persevere in our marriage, in our family life and with the field of difficulties with which we are familiar in our work. In other words, the call to faith is not a magical act of "wishing away" the daily obstacles to our various goals - no matter how much we may want this; rather, the call to faith is that persevering dialogue with God in the midst of everything that is going on, with each person we know and with what contact we have with the problems in the world.

A Final Word

I, like anyone else, fall many times in the course of being the person God makes it possible for me to be; and, in a particular way, the call of the writer is to use words to help: to help to heal the many ways that words have wounded and continue to wound. Therefore the last word goes to a fairly recent poem.

It is about writing in such a way as the stages of hurt are both articulated and, at the same time, softened in the expression; indeed, words can burrow in under the guise of being pleasant and, as it were, a tone of voice or a deceiving smile can leave them, like a melted spike, as an indescribable pain that seeps through the psyche needing an antidote.

In the final line there is a reference to 'the truth that heals', which went on to inspire two of the pieces that comprise this anthology on pilgrimage; indeed, in their own way, they are about that realism which describes, really, that our salvation is no fiction and takes a life-time to be real.

Bruised or Well-used Words?

When the heart spikes and the tongue spits
words through the bashing impact of pain,
bruised words which disfigure the still discolouring wound,
– bearing the blunt hurt
they bludgeon understanding and aggravate grief.

Left for a while, these prayed,
aggravated insights evict the venom within,
becoming middling words,
like an arrow pulled from the wound,
too fresh to be anything but singularly painful;
and yet, the point pulled,
they start drawing the unforgiving infection:

the rebellion; the protest; and the vengeful bite.

Fiction or fact, there is "within and between"
the truth told in different ways, an exploration,

now in human history,

now in an account that goes to places where the heart,

perhaps too painfully pierced,

is visited more easily by a stranger to the original experience.

But well used words, softly saying what hurts but helps,
alight like butterflies, almost too gently to be noticed,
trailing evidence of passing into thought the word which
opens the heart to the Word within the word,
which knows the words we need
to hear the truth that heals.

Postscript

An Evangelizing Fool for God

This is a piece about the history of marriage being integral to the evangelical mission: that marriage belongs to the pilgrim process of announcing to others the saving action of God. In other words, there are times when it is possible to experience, intensely, as it were, being in the midst of others and hoping in the help to them of witnessing to what God has done. This is a brief account, then, of going two by two in the context of a world-wide mission of evangelisation; and, as such, announcing the love and experience of God and not, as such, a particular charism of the Catholic Church.

Three Personal Facts

Owing to clots in the legs and blood leaking from the valves into the bottom of my legs, the vascular surgeon had said that, unlikely as it was, it would do me good to walk a lot. On the two by two, my companion and I were sent into a big city, without phones or money, and over the course of a week we walked over sixty miles! I had also begun a course of antibiotics for a bladder infection. But, providentially, being sent into the city provided the help that I needed. Just as we were turning away from a presbytery, thinking that at ten thirty it was too late to find hospitality, a priest opened the door to show his friend out and, in the same moment, I came back from half-way down the street and announced that we were there to share what God had done for us. The parish priest was called and my companion and I were invited in and given a floor for the week.

On the Wednesday before we had even left for this Gathering or Convivance, a weekend together with around one hundred and fifty others which was to prepare us for going on the two by two, I was present at a Liturgy of the Word and I prayed for an opportunity to sit, alone and in silence, and to pray for all the different needs that were pressing upon me. On the two by two there were many opportunities to sit, alone and in silence, and to pray.

It was also a difficult time for me to do the two by two. On the one hand seven of our eight children were home with my wife, with the eighth returning home; and then, the following week, they went on holiday, without me, with the rest of my wife's family. On the other hand, I had been criticised for leaving my wife with the children and others thought that I was not well enough to go. My wife, however, was willing for me to go; and, therefore, one of my objectives was to pray for my wife and children constantly. Coming back from the two by two my wife and I found that we experienced a new closeness in being together and that it was possible for me to spend more, much needed time, talking with my children.

The First of the Two Gatherings or Convivances: Before the Two by Two

We came to the first gathering of "would-be" evangelists, from the 21st to the 23rd July, to be sent by Christ and the Church to go and announce the love of God for sinners, inviting others to listen to our experience and to share their own. Just as Christ sent his disciples two by two, and just as the Church has continued this tradition, so we were sent two by two: two men or two women. The weekend began and ended in the context of the prayer of the Church, a Penitential rite with personal confession and the celebration of the Eucharist.

Each two, and their destination, were chosen at random. I was delighted to find that my companion was from the North of England and, at the same time, knew the capital very well as he had been a taxi driver. When it was time to leave, we decided to be "simple" and to go to Westminster Cathedral to begin our mission with a blessing from a Bishop and to see what unfolded for us by beginning to visit the Catholic Churches on our list. Although I had imagined that I would pack my rucksack with as much additional "stuff" as I could, including pajamas, dressing gown and toilet paper, after listening to a letter from a sister in China who had already done the two by two, I decided to do the opposite: to take out everything from my rucksack, except the cream for my legs, bible, cross, rosary and to trust more in Providence than what I could quash into what was, anyway, a very small bag. As a part of the preparatory Convivance, we were given all kinds of practical suggestions about where to sleep and to eat if we were not offered hospitality; and, at the same time, we were encouraged not to judge anyone and to offer any hardships or difficulties for those we met.

One further point, I was thinking of wearing a T-shirt with an image of Christ on the Cross and the words: "Father, forgive them". Reluctant to wear this T-shirt and to look like a walking "bill-board", I nevertheless decided to do this as a part of the whole experience. As the week of the two by two went on and we walked through hundreds and thousands of people in central London and various other places in Marylebone, Camden and Islington, it was a humbling experience being "a fool for God" in this T-shirt.

Specific Moments in the Whole Experience of the Two by Two

We were invited to begin our mission with a prayer from the highest place that we could find; and, therefore, we went to the BT-tower, but were refused entry. The priest who gave us hospitality suggested that we go to the tower at Westminster Cathedral. After explaining that we had no money and that we wanted to pray for London, we were refused entry to the Westminster tower and thus we went and sat and prayed. While looking for a toilet we called in at a Catholic book shop and asked for a drink of water and the use of their toilets; and, after seeing my T-shirt, I was asked if we were on the two by two and we were given a drink, lunch and the exact money for the tower. We were then given the tickets to the tower at a reduced rate and donated the difference to the cathedral.

My companion and I decided, in view of the long walks between

Catholic Churches, to call at random on any denomination that we passed; and, in addition, we called at a Synagogue that was not far from the floor on which we slept. After calling at the Synagogue and explaining that we are Christians on a week of evangelization and that we would like to pray in the place of worship of the people who expressed, for us, the history of salvation, we were invited to return the following day, which we did. Although this was a relatively brief visit, we learnt that the Synagogue originated from the temporary structure in which God dwelt during the forty years in the desert and, at the same time, we saw a wonderful, double-door sized Tabernacle of the Word, the Torah, the Jewish tradition of which had clearly influenced the Neocatechumenal use of a Tabernacle for the Word of God. I recalled the Biblical Hebrew for the opening line of Genesis, explaining how this word was a turning point for me at forty – in front of being unable to marry or to do anything with my life except consider suicide or sin. Because if God could create everything out of nothing He could make a new beginning for the sinner, which was me[143]. I also shared the "moment" of hope that I experienced when, on passing through Auschwitz-Birkenau, it was clearly a ruin: a memorial to the suffering experienced. Our host said that the last time he visited the concentration camp was thirty years ago, to which my companion replied that at that time, under communism, there had been no mention of the Jews. Unexpectedly, our host said, perhaps it was time he went again. We thanked our host warmly and left.

One evening, about seven thirty, we were looking for a place to do Evening Prayer and we found an open Anglican Church. I asked

---

143 See the *Catechism of the Catholic Church*, 298.

the vicar, who was about to celebrate a Communion Service in a side chapel, if we could pray in the back of the Church. He allowed us to do this but I declined the invitation to attend the Service; indeed, I said, God would draw good from our different prayers. My companion saw a notice that explained the vicar was going to move, shortly, to another parish with his husband. We were there neither to argue nor to judge. At the end of our prayers, we spoke briefly with him of the love of God, as he had a meeting to go to; and, even in response to these few words, he said it was a very good message and left. We visited many Anglican as well as Catholic parishes, a Quaker Meeting House, a Greek Orthodox Church and an Ethiopian Coptic Church; and, whether briefly or at length, we witnessed to how God manifested His love for us in the concrete events of our lives. Occasionally we met people who did not understand what we were doing or thought it was about promoting the Neocatechumenal Way; but, wherever we went, we invited people to listen to our experience of the love of God for sinners, beginning with ourselves, and we prayed for whoever we met and offered whatever we experienced for those we encountered. One of our most moving visits was with a Catholic priest who, after forty years of priestly ministry, was almost in tears as he explained that he had experienced that without Christ he could do absolutely nothing.

In the end, it was particularly clear how the word of God, in the Holy Scripture, enlightened us about our lives and that, in general, what we needed was to listen to it. Many people, on reflection, were touched by the fact that just as Christ came with a word at the Marriage Feast of Cana, so He came at the very beginning of my married life. In other words, Christ did not wait to heal the wounds of sin, He came in the very celebration of the sacrament of marriage to convert water into wine! Indeed, it is almost central to the vocation to marriage to give witness to Christ's constant transformation of sufferings into celebrations: water into wine.

In general, providence gave us both what we needed. My companion had been sent to China to evangelise, over eighteen months ago, and that because of the routine scanning of kidneys it was discovered that he had kidney cancer. Because this is not a routine procedure in this country, normally kidney cancer is not discovered until it is too late to be helpful and the person dies. My companion, we can say, was saved by the providence of God sending him to China where his cancer was diagnosed and he was operated on successfully on his immediate return to England. The walking we did helped him to see, too, that he was far fitter than he realised.

The Second of the Two Gatherings or Convivances: After the Two by Two

On our return, the head of the team who had organized the whole event washed my feet, saying that he did it out of love for the announcement of the Gospel. This was completely unexpected and I wept on his shoulder. The second Convivance was dedicated to listening to everyone's experience of the two by two. Although the two by two was a world-wide event over the summer months, my impression was that this was an important "moment" in the evangelization of England and Wales: a kind of stimulus to Christian, interreligious dialogue and dialogue with anyone and everyone. One visit to a Mosque elicited the response from an

Imam that there needed to be more occasions of this kind of dialogue. Even though the event was not deliberately ecumenical, clearly God intended it to be taken up by a variety of Christian denominations and faiths.

As we returned to the meeting room provided for our use and sat in front of the Icons which were a part of the liturgical accompaniment to the whole experience, the Icon which caught my attention more and more was an image of Christ on the cross. My longing to be with my family and the delays due to "handing back" the experience of the two by two to the communities from which we came, who had accompanied us with their prayers and other acts, only intensified this suffering. At the same time I prayed about the many failures in my life and the constant call to faith in God. What was unexpected and thought-provoking, then, was the impression of Christ being happy on the cross. This image was a focus of my meditation, both then and since, as it has become a real part of my dialogue with Christ to be happy amidst the difficulties, stresses and busyness of being married and having eight children, from nine to twenty; indeed, although life has been incredibly hectic since my return, with both one of the children's cousins staying with us for a few days, a Spanish youth for nearly a month and all the coming and going of an active family, I would say that there is a new openness between my children and myself. What is more, my wife has remarked on being "more loved" since my return from the two by two.

The whole passage, from leaving my family and being on the two by two, was like the Easter Triduum: beginning with the heart ache of leaving my family. Then there was entering the Holy Saturday experience of the "silence" of being "phone-less", accentuated when we returned and, little by little, I heard how it was going with my wife and children. The third part of this *Triduum* was, then, about recognizing that my experience of the two by two was far humbler than many other accounts and, along with acknowledging my imperfections as a husband, parent and Christian, my prayer became simpler still: asking God continually to do what I could not do. On the Wednesday morning, then, before the final Eucharist and our departure, I awoke conscious of being happy in front of the word of Christ: I died and rose for you!

www.ingramcontent.com/pod-product-compliance
Lightning Source LLC
Chambersburg PA
CBHW031830090426
42741CB00005B/188
* 9 7 8 1 7 3 2 4 1 4 8 3 9 *